WELCOME TO THE DIFFICULT YEARS.
NOW WHAT DO YOU DO?

Your child has just come home with her third unsatisfactory math test in a row! What do you do?

In THE MIDDLE SCHOOL YEARS, Michele A. Hernández provides a detailed, comprehensive checklist that parents should follow to help their child achieve better grades at school. From setting up the right workplace to helping a child organize his or her notebook, it all adds up. And if your child is still having trouble with a class or classes, this book tells you what to do next.

• • •

Your child says he hates his teacher. What do you do?

Michele Hernández urges you to get more specific information from your child and talk to other parents. When you have all the facts you need, go to school. But know who to talk to first.

• • •

Your child wants to do more extracurricular activities. You're worried about grades. What do you do?

The answer may surprise you. THE MIDDLE SCHOOL YEARS advocates an integrated approach to your child's education that takes into account the need for exploration and outside activities. And these activities may pay off when it comes to applying for college.

THE MIDDLE SCHOOL YEARS

ACHIEVING THE BEST EDUCATION FOR YOUR CHILD GRADES 5–8

MICHELE A. HERNÁNDEZ

WARNER BOOKS

A Time Warner Company

MT

Warner Books, Inc., 1271 Avenue of the Americas, New York, NY 10020

Visit our Web site at www.twbookmark.com

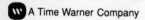 A Time Warner Company

Printed in the United States of America
First Printing: July 2000
10 9 8 7 6 5 4 3 2

Library of Congress Cataloging-in-Publication Data
Hernández, Michele A.
   The middle school years : achieving the best education for your child, grades 5–8 /
Michele A. Hernández.
      p. cm.
   Includes bibliographical references and index.
   ISBN 0-446-67562-8
   1. Middle school education.   2. Middle school education—Parent participation.
I. Title.
LB1623.H466 2000
373.236—dc21   99-086717

Book design by Charles Sutherland
Cover design by Mary Ann Smith
Cover photograph by © David Young—Wolff/Tony Stone Image

12/10/03

*To my family and friends and all the
inspirational teachers I have studied with
and befriended over the years.*

Contents

Author's Note

You've already taken the first concrete, positive step in working with your children to develop a set of skills and the right attitude to make them successful in and out of school. The fact that you are reading this book says that you are a concerned parent who wants only the best experience for your children. You are on the right track to helping your children gain a sense of self-confidence and helping them achieve their academic potential. My goal is simply to help you teach your children how to succeed academically without putting undue stress on them.

Acknowledgments

First off, I would like to thank my aunt, Susan Banks, who gave me a blueprint for what parents needed to know and then read several drafts of the book to make suggestions and corrections. I should also thank, Michael Banks, for being the "guinea pig," as he was going through eighth grade at Horace Mann at the time.

My utmost gratitude to the hundreds of parents at my current school who took the time to fill out my survey that asked them to comment on what kind of information they felt was lacking both at our school and in schools in general. Their comments, phone calls, conferences, and suggestions are incorporated throughout the book. Special thanks to many of the brilliant students in my honors English class who volunteered study tips in the chapter entitled Egghead Tips for Success: Alex Lee, Eddie Buonopane, Jeff Renard, Jason Green-Lowe, Jason Margolin, and Natalie Karabel. I know I'll be reading their books someday.

Many administrators were tremendously helpful at specific points during the book's writing. I would like to thank my close friend and colleague Bruce Bayliss for lending me his more than 25 years of educational experiences both in the U.S. and overseas. His constant day-to-day support kept me going many days when coffee failed. He was one of the only souls brave enough to read through the entire manuscript and make uncounted suggestions and additions, all of which strengthened the final product. Gregg Goldberg also deserves thanks for both his wealth of educational knowledge and his grammatical and literary expertise. Thanks to Les Gordon and Norma Blackman for help on the learning disabilities chapter, to Stephanie Block for her educational musings and to Mary Anne Fraser who contributed to Appendix D. One parent, Robert Katz, was particularly helpful since he took the time to read an early draft and make literally hundreds of comments and suggestions. Finally, thanks to the "voice" of the school, Mary Ann Holck, who not only maintains her calm all day talking to parents, but also was tremendously helpful in seeing that manuscript copies were sent on time.

My old friend "reader extraordinaire" Phyllis Wharton once again gave me endless amounts of support and input—because she always gives her most honest opinion, she forced me to be merciless in editing out any information that was either unclear or superfluous. Heartfelt thanks to Francis Jalet Miller from Warner who probably put more time in at every phase than anyone. Because of her incisive editing, commentary, and ability to send double-digit pages of faxes, the book is much stronger than it would have been otherwise. Two of my high school teachers, Bud Pollak and Sandra Abt, deserve mention for their advice and help not just on this book, but also on educational issues in general throughout the years of our long friendship.

A warm thanks to everyone at Warner Books: Karen Thompson did a fantastic job on the copy editing; Senior Editor Rick Wolff, as always, inspired me to hit deadlines at the speed of light; Eric Wechter put up with all my last-minute changes and Rick's assistant Dan Ambrosio answered all my anxious phone calls during the year. Of course, my agent and friend Robin Straus supported me the whole way through this project and lent her vision and expertise to the project as well as some guinea pigs of her own. Finally, thanks to my parents, my sister Jennifer, and my daughter Alexia.

Introduction

One of the biggest errors we parents make is that we feel it is the school's job to educate our children. Granted, we have some fantastic middle schools, high schools, and universities in our country, but even the finest of these cannot be solely responsible for educating our children.

Too often we turn our children over to the schools and pray for the best. It's interesting to see how a country like Japan looks upon childhood development: Japanese parents regard ages one through five as the easy part of childhood when they can focus on playing with and enjoying their children, but once school starts at age five, they believe the hard work begins. In other words, once school starts, the heat is on and the work begins for parents, whose job it is to help their children excel in school.

This book teaches parents how to exert a certain measure of control over their children's education in a way that works along with schools in educating their children. It also will teach parents to be proactive at every level so that they avoid problems before they develop. Education starts at home—no school can by itself turn a totally nonmotivated and noninquiring student into a young Ben Franklin. The more quickly we realize that in some sense all parents "home-school" their children, the sooner we will realize that our role as parents is paramount.

If there is any problem with our school system, it is the communication gap that exists between the school and the parents. Often parents ask, "How was school today?" and the child responds, "Fine." Until the child comes home with a bad report card, most parents would take their child's word at face value and believe that all really was fine.

Think about it from the child's vantage point: It is the rare middle school child who, after struggling in many classes throughout the day, will respond to the above question, "Well, actually, I have no idea what's going on in math, I'm having trouble with reading comprehension so I can't even keep up with my reading in English class, and I seem to have an auditory processing problem that keeps me in the dark during class."

In fact, the more trouble a child is having, particularly a young child, the less likely he is to tell his parents unless asked a specific question. By contrast, a successful student tends to respond to a general question by giving a blow-by-blow account of everything he has learned that day, although that enthusiasm tapers off a bit in middle school. Teenagers can get a bit tight-lipped about school as they get older!

How can you as parents bridge the gap between your child and the school? This book teaches you, step by step, not only how to prepare your child for success, but also how to stay abreast of his school progress in middle school and high school. It also will advise you when it's appropriate to intervene and when it's better to step back from the situation.

Middle school is the perfect time to work out the boundaries of your relationship to your child's education. As I will argue, perhaps the best way to define a parent's role in this relationship is as that of a *steward*—one who guides the child during the younger years but imparts enough lifetime skills so that the child can survive and flourish without the mentor or steward by late middle school or early high school.

The situation is analogous in a fanciful way to animals that raise their offspring in the wild. Small animals are dependent upon their mothers while they are young, but within a short time they learn all the skills they need to survive in the wild. The animal that becomes too dependent on the mother will die in the wild if it is separated from her. Of course we don't need to run the analogy into the ground, but the point is relevant: You don't want to do things *for* your child because you are only making it more difficult for him to become independent, a process that should be a major goal of adolescents who are on their way to becoming adults. On the one hand, you need to begin this steward role in late elementary school or early middle school, but on the other hand, if you wait until high school to help your children learn how to be independent, it will often be too late. As is the case with many areas of life, timing is everything.

I write this book largely for parents of middle school and high school students. You will learn how to be advocates for your children, how to teach them to become self-sufficient as students, and how to motivate them to achieve at their highest level.

Every child has his own special talents—art, music, math, computers, hockey, and so on. Let me be clear that this book emphasizes a child's achievement relative to his particular abilities. It does not promise miracles; it cannot, for example, take a child with an extremely low aptitude in math and turn him into Isaac Newton. What it will do is help you to recognize and nurture your child's talents while at the same time helping him to overcome the many obstacles and stumbling blocks he will face throughout his education.

As any of you who have raised adolescents know, the period from around sixth grade to tenth grade is an incredibly difficult time for students in terms of social, intellectual, and physical development. Rarely will a sane parent refer to the middle school years as a favorite developmental stage. This book will help you get through this difficult period with flying colors by raising your child's self-esteem, teaching him study and organizational skills, and, most importantly, teaching him to be his own advocate in high school and beyond.

This last point is a crucial one and reiterates what I said earlier about serving a steward role: When our children are in elementary and middle school, it is our responsibility to be their advocates and to teach them how to study, why to study, and how to achieve to the best of their ability. However, we fail if our children become so dependent on us that they cannot go to college without bringing us in their suitcases.

The old proverb "Catch a fish for me and I eat for a day;

show me how to fish and I eat for a lifetime" captures this philosophy quite well. Our goal is to teach our children all the necessary skills so that they will become independent enough to succeed on their own in high school, in college, and beyond. Therefore, all the chapters herein lead parents step by step through this process of educating their children at home.

Though the information is quite specific, it is general enough to be used by parents and teachers from all different parts of the country, from private and public school systems alike. I address many issues that pertain to both public and private schools, occasionally pausing to differentiate between the two when the need arises.

One final caution: We want to avoid falling into the trap that many parents do of trying to lead our lives through our children. It is critical to separate your life from your child's and to let him lead his own life and follow his own talents and callings. If you try to mold your children into what you think they should be like, you will only discourage them and squash their own natural talents.

With these goals in mind, let us turn to the most important stumbling block for students at all levels: how to help them *organize* their lives so they know what it is they need to do in order to succeed.

Chapter 1

Organization 101: Teaching Your Child How to Get His Act Together

Before setting out to design a book that would be helpful for both parents and students, I sent out a survey to roughly 650 parents at the private school where I work. I asked them a series of questions about education: what skills they felt their children lacked, what they wished the schools would teach, and what they already did in order to help their children. I grouped all these questions into different subject areas and outlined the book's major chapters around parents' most pressing concerns.

My biggest surprise was that an overwhelming number of parents (about 80 percent of those surveyed) said they felt that their children's most serious problem was a total lack of organizational skills: how to organize a locker, a backpack, a notebook, a schedule—the list went on and on. Most parents wished that the school had a larger role in teaching these skills but acknowledged that they wished they were better informed to help their children learn these vital skills at home.

Since I monitor the academic progress of all students on our campus (high school and middle school), I have the opportunity to speak to many parents every day about their children's academic struggles. In the majority of cases, their academic problems are rooted in their inability to organize their time, their workload, and their various after-school commitments, rather than in any lack of academic talent. The more time I spend in schools, the more clear it is to me that a student who learns to be a master of his own schedule is much more likely to succeed than an equally bright student who is organizationally impaired.

Why is it that young middle school students have such difficulty organizing their lives? The hardest adjustment for young children is the transition from having the same teacher all day (as most do in elementary school) to having a different teacher for every subject (the norm for middle school). More than any other factor, this dramatic procedural change marks the transition from the comforting environment of elementary school to the often "sink-or-swim" environment of middle school.

Think of the change from your child's perspective: Children love predictability and regularity. For years they have been accustomed to having the same person teach them all day, almost always in the same room. They have had time to learn that teacher's idiosyncrasies: Does she write the assignments on the board? On a piece of paper that goes home to parents? Whatever the case may be, they quickly adapt to the teacher's methods, and through sheer repetition, become more or less adept at keeping track of assignments.

Suddenly, at the onset of sixth grade, students may find themselves in a different location (some schools switch campuses after the fifth grade), while at the same time their routine is completely disrupted. Not only do they have a different teacher for every subject, they also have to move physically from classroom to classroom—the teachers do not come to them. Add to that the confusion of five different ways of assigning homework in the best of cases; that is, assuming each of the teachers is consistent in using the same technique every day. Is it any wonder, then, that many children who were doing fine in elementary school find themselves lost and confused when they get to middle school?

When your children make the transition from fifth to sixth grade (or from sixth to seventh grade), it is perfectly okay as parents to help them organize themselves and teach them the necessary skills.

In some schools, the teachers themselves teach organizational skills, but in my experience, the majority of students in the United States do not learn them well enough, or shall we say early enough, to help them succeed before they get too far behind.

I think it's better to assume that whatever methods they learn in school, while not necessarily incorrect, will just scratch the surface of what I will try to outline for you here. As a postscript, although you should help your children learn these study skills yourself, you should also put pressure on the school to teach them as well. Many fine schools devote an entire class to study and organizational skills because they don't count on individual teachers' being able to cover all the skills students will need to succeed.

The first thing your child will need is the proper set of school supplies. Of course these supplies vary greatly from school to school, and even from teacher to teacher. I don't want to devote a great deal of space to school supplies in this chapter, but if you want a quick refresher course, I have included information on backpacks, binders, paper, homework notebooks, and basic school supplies in Appendix B at the back of this book. Feel free to flip through this section if you need to.

Homework Notebook

There is one item so valuable that I will discuss it here in greater detail than I do in Appendix B, and that is the homework notebook. There is no general agreement as to whether the homework notebook should be a little tiny notepad, a calendar-sized daily planner, or a full-sized notebook, but I do think it should be its own separate entity and not simply a section of the three-ring binder. I say this because the three-ring binder is a big, clunky item that no child is going to want to take out of his bookbag if he doesn't have to. Imagine: The class is just ending, your child has already put his big notebook away, but suddenly the teacher says, "Whoops, I almost forgot—be sure to do exercises one through ten in your grammar book." If it's a choice of dragging out the binder or just saying to himself "Oh, I'll remember . . ." (which has an almost zero probability), he will probably opt for the latter. On the other hand, if your child has a smaller and more easily accessible notebook, he is much more likely simply to pull it out of his backpack and copy down the homework assignment.

At least while your child is a sixth- and seventh-grader, I would recommend organizing the notebook *with* him (not *for* him) so that you train him well and leave him with a lifetime of good study skills and habits. Before school starts, suggest that your child design a chart for each week of the first few months of school. This chart can be formatted in any number of ways, but you want to be sure to have the dates and days of the week in the left column with a few spaces between each one, and a place for all five subjects across the top. If the notebook is shaped like a rectangle, have your child use the short side for the days and dates and the long side for the subjects. A sample notebook might look like this:

	Math	Lang. Arts	Spanish	Social Studies	Science
Monday 9/1 Books Needed:					
Tuesday 9/2 Books:					
Wed. 9/3 Books:					
Thurs. 9/4 Books:					
Friday 9/5 Books:					

Once you have taken the time to set up this notebook with your child, the important part of the routine is to check it every day for the first week of school to make sure that your child is in fact writing down every assignment. After that week, tell your child in a nice way that you reserve the right to check his homework notebook at any time.

I think the hardest statement for parents to deal with is "But Mom, I don't have any homework." To get around this fabrication, I would require that your child fill out the whole chart every day. If there is no homework for a certain class, you should have him write in "No homework" rather than just leaving the space blank. That way you can at least check with a particular teacher if you see a pattern of not writing down the homework.

A major advantage of a calendar-style planner (available at stationery stores, or any office-supply store like Office Max, Staples, or Office Depot) is the ability to "log in" the future due dates of long-range assignments, term papers, exam dates, et cetera.

Although setting up a homework notebook seems simple, I can almost guarantee that children who get into the habit of keeping close track of all assignments early on will be much more successful students than those who rely on memory or on asking other students in the class.

With technology becoming even more accessible in classrooms across the country, some schools have Web pages that can be accessed at home and at school so teachers can post their nightly homework for all to see. If your school does this, it is a great backup method to compare your child's written homework notebook with the Web syllabus so you can have the most updated information.

You need to impress upon your child the importance of taking a minute toward the end of the school day to look at the night's homework assignments so he can figure out which books he will need to bring home. In fact, it is a very good idea, at least in the younger grades, to have your child add a column to the homework pad that reads "Books needed" so that he can quickly scan down and figure out that he can't do his math homework without the math textbook, for example. Although it sounds painfully obvious, anyone who has had kids or dealt with students on a daily basis knows that one of the most common excuses for not being able to do homework is "Oh, I can't do my reading because I left the book in school."

At the very least, students need to bring home all notebooks (the three-ring binder, the homework notebook, plus math or any other subject that has one) and then the appropriate textbooks. Finally, you might want to make it a rule that loose pieces of paper have no place in the backpack since they only get ripped to shreds or lost. At least while your children are young, you may want to check their backpacks every few days to make sure there is some order and neatness. No need to nag them; just let them know you reserve the right to check their backpack periodically. Insist that once homework assignments are completed, they must be clipped back into the binder or, in the case of a spiral notebook, into a folder for that subject so that they are not floating around in the backpack.

One further note about going through your child's backpack: By the time a child is in sixth grade, he has the right of privacy. Therefore you should assure your child that you will not read personal notes from his friends or go through his notebook page by page.

Leaving Books in School

There are ways to reduce the risk of your children leaving books in school. One extreme measure is to buy an extra copy of the heaviest, bulkiest textbooks to keep at home; yet this is costly and many public schools don't even have enough to go around in the first place. However, even if you can't afford to buy an extra textbook, there is another way at least to minimize the number of days a week your child will need to carry the book home. Assuming that the teacher is organized and assigns work in advance, if your child brings home the textbook for a certain subject on a Friday, he can actually complete the assignments for Monday, Tuesday, and Wednesday of the following week so that he does not necessarily need to bring the book home unless there is a test that needs to be studied for. As we will see in later chapters, getting ahead or reading ahead in several subjects is one of the keys for later academic success.

Some teachers allow students to use a "buddy system" rather than transport back and forth five or six heavy textbooks every day: Two buddy students bring a certain heavy textbook to school on alternate days, and then they sit next to each other in the classroom so they can share their class copy.

If you actually pick up your child at school every day (and I realize that the majority of students will take the bus, but this advice is for those who don't), there is no excuse to leave a book at school because you can remind your child to check which books will be necessary to complete the night's homework before you leave the campus. Finally, money permitting, it's not a bad idea to invest in a basic fax machine (around $150 to $200) so students in your children's class can fax any missed assignments. Many reasonably priced fax machines also have a copying capability; you'd be surprised how often your child will need to photocopy something that is homework related!

Missing School

One thing you will need to teach your children early on is that if they miss school for any reason, it is their responsibility to find out what the homework was. If you know your child is home sick for the day, remind him to call teachers himself for the assignments if he's well enough to do the homework. Good teachers expect to be called and often call home if they know a child is sick (if they don't have a huge class load like many public-school teachers, a situation that makes a phone call home almost an impossibility). If it is hard to reach the teachers at the school, your child should compile a list at the beginning of each school year of two children in each of his classes with their phone numbers. These children can either be friends or just very bright and reliable children (most teachers would be happy to recommend a student who they know always does the homework so that they don't have to be called every time someone misses school). After the school day, you should encourage your child to call this list (hopefully we are only talking about one or two calls, since usually children share several classes) to find out: (1) what they did in every class that day and (2) what the homework is.

There will be cases when your child really can't do the homework because the lesson is impossible without the class instruction, but at the very least the child should attempt it in order to have an idea of what was covered so that he does not feel hopelessly behind when he returns to school. Once your child returns to school, you should train him to talk to every single teacher to explain why he was absent and to ask how he can make up the work. This kind of responsibility at an early age impresses teachers and also prepares students for the years of school ahead. It also teaches them the lesson that missing school does not mean missing work or being allowed to skip something; in fact, it means doing *more* work to make up what was missed.

The Locker

The only topic we have not covered that has to do with organization is the school locker, assuming your school is like most and has lockers. In terms of developing a procedure, it is a good idea to give your children sometime at beginning of sixth grade a quick lesson in organizing their locker at the beginning of the day. Their first step is making an extra copy of their schedule so that one copy stays in their notebook at all times and the other can be posted right inside the locker's door. This way, your child never loses track of exactly where he is supposed to be at any given time of day.

Next, your child should empty his backpack and impose some order: perhaps textbooks in one section of the locker and notebooks in another. Then the backpack can be hung up for the day on a hook and your child can carry all books he will need before lunch in his arms, then all books he will need after lunch in the second load (if the locker is centrally located). On those occasions when parents are invited into the school for parent-teacher conferences or for open-school nights, it is a good idea to glance inside your child's locker to get a sense of how well he is organizing himself; that is, no loose papers, no rampant disorganization or sloppiness.

Although it may seem like a lot of work on your part to help your children learn how to organize their school days, children carry these habits with them for the rest of their school lives and beyond, so that you will not have to repeat every step every year. Once your children have the organizational tools for success, your job shifts from organizational coach to progress checker, so that all you have to do is touch base once or twice a week to make sure that homework is getting done and that your child is upholding his side of the bargain in school.

Now that we have covered these basic organizational skills, we turn to the crucial process of creating an environment at home that encourages students to succeed academically.

Chapter 2

How to Create an Academic Environment at Home

The Work Space

It is never too early to reinforce the fact that learning is important. For example, the best thing you can do for your children, starting from when they are two or three years old, is to read to them, and to let them see you reading in your leisure time. From what we know of child psychology, children are constantly looking to model their behavior on yours, so if they have positive childhood memories of everyone sitting around on the bed or in the living room reading they will associate reading with intimacy, support, family togetherness, and security.

In my years working in highly selective admissions at Dartmouth College, I read thousands of applications, but very few had SAT verbal scores of 800 (out of 800) or close to that. In every single case, the student who earned a perfect 800 was a voracious reader. Many of them wrote their college essays about their own childhood memories of reading and how it made them feel close to their parents since they were able to enjoy time together reading and sharing their experiences.

What we need to consider is how you can instill in your child a love of reading and how you can use a similar method so that he enjoys doing his homework. The key is that you must try to create a positive environment in the home, a special place where children can think, read quietly, and do homework without too many distractions. Ideally, it would be better to use a room other than the bedroom (since the bedroom is where your child can express himself: He might have a stereo, posters of rock singers, books, musical instruments, stuffed animals, all of which serve as distractions and mental escapes from the task at hand), but many of us do not have the luxury of having extra rooms. In fact, in the majority of cases, two siblings share the same bedroom and the rest of the house is small, so the key is to set boundaries for the bedroom, like keeping music and television off during homework time. Children who try to watch TV or listen to loud music while doing homework usually fail because they cannot absorb so many stimuli at the same time.

The bottom line is that the location of the physical place itself is not that important and depends mostly on how your house is laid out. You want it to be a quiet space (i.e., not next to a window by a busy street, not next to a very loud dishwasher or a telephone where you will be talking while your child is working), with good ventilation. It should have a reasonably big table or desk where a student can spread out his books and everything he needs within arm's length. A good choice, besides the bedroom, would be a library or den, or any room that has books or other academic material already nearby.

Last but not least, even if the ambient lighting is pretty good, I would recommend investing in a halogen desk lamp (you can buy them now for between ten and twenty dollars at many office-supply stores) so that your child will not have to strain his eyes while trying to read. If a child has trouble seeing what he is reading, it will give him a headache, make him impatient to finish, and only create bad associations with doing homework in the first place. Children will never answer yes to the parental query, "Don't you need more light?" so you need to be vigilant on their behalf. Also, a comfortable chair is a good idea because it makes the process of sitting down and studying a more pleasant one.

The Routine

Children need routine in their lives, particularly in regard to doing homework and getting used to a schedule. Remember, it is always easy when they get older to allow more freedom, but while they are young, you want to mold their behavior as much as you can to teach them positive habits.

Assuming your child gets home from school around three or four o'clock (this could be later if they have extracurricular activities on certain days), the first thing you should do is allow him to have a healthy snack so that his brain has some energy. High-fat foods like potato chips or nacho chips are not recommended because they do not provide as much energy to the brain as a healthier, more substantial snack. If you set children to work on an empty stomach, they will be much less productive and much less able to concentrate.

Once they have had some juice (or lots of water), and non-junk food, you need to set the routine: They will take their books to the designated study room and work on homework either until it is completed, or for at least thirty minutes, at which point a break is in order before resuming again. Obviously, by the time they reach high school, they might find themselves with three to five hours of homework, but by then they will automatically schedule in their own breaks when they are tired and resume when they are ready. Until they mature to that level, it's better to have a strict plan with some enticing rewards at the end.

I think it's important to emphasize to children that homework is a fun and useful activity, not something to dash through so that they can watch TV. Completion of homework leads to positive reinforcement (from the teacher and from classmates) and fulfillment in class; once the child starts to achieve this success, it will naturally lead to more reinforcement and greater success. How does a parent create the impression that homework is important? I think primarily by showing interest in what the child is doing. Ask what he is studying in each subject and try to ask some questions that show that you are either familiar with the topic or would like to find out more. Let's say they are studying adding and subtracting and accounting, and you never for the life of you could figure out how to do this well. You could ask them to show you what they've learned and add something like, "Now that you've shown me that, I'll finally be able to balance my checkbook more accurately."

What you've done is made some seemingly irrelevant thing they are learning in school into something that has importance in everyday life. The same goes for science, history, and all other subjects, academic and otherwise.

If you happen to know a lot about a certain area, let's say English, you might want to discuss the book they are reading and ask them some questions about it. "I loved that book when I first read it; I remember that my grandfather read it out loud to me when I spent the summer in Maine." By bringing your own life experiences to their schoolwork, you are positively reinforcing that what children are learning is not just useless busywork, but rather is information that is vital to their lives: This is a big step in the right direction.

As for positive rewards for finishing homework, that will depend on what your child likes to do in his spare time. If his passion is playing catch with the neighbors, that is the carrot you would dangle; if he prefers to play with his train set, then you would offer that option instead. In fact, especially when they are young, I think you could encourage children to do almost anything they wanted to as long as all homework is done.

A word of caution: You should be the one, at least while your child is learning a routine, to follow up and check whether homework is really done. Spot checks are a helpful idea. Every few days ask to see the homework notebook and have your child give you a brief synopsis of what is to be completed. That should help you gauge how long he should spend on one area and whether he is on track. If your child says that he has to read four chapters of *To Kill a Mockingbird*, it will be a good guess that most of the homework for that evening is reading.

In addition, spot checks will help you help your child get ahead. If when you check the homework assignments, there is no reading for Monday night but you notice that he has to be on page 124 of *To Kill a Mockingbird* by Thursday, you need to help your child divide up the reading load so he can break it down into smaller daily segments. Until your child becomes proficient at breaking down tasks, I think it is your job as a parent at least to teach the skill so that your child will be able to do it on his own well-managed segments of time.

I'd like to insert a friendly reminder at this point: You need to do all this in a loving way, not a nagging way. At all costs, you want to avoid a situation where you are forcing your child at gunpoint to do his work. That's why it's always important to reinforce the subject material as I've described above.

Why Not Every Child Should Go to Harvard! How Not to Turn the Heat Up Too High

Some other cautionary words: You as a parent are trying to set up a routine so that your child has all the tools necessary to succeed, but, as I noted in the introduction, success is a relative term. Much depends on the ability level of your child. Keep in mind these words of wisdom: Not everyone can or even should attend a highly selective college.

What you really want to encourage is that your child try his hardest so you are confident he is succeeding to the best of *his* ability level. If you see that your child has had difficulty in math for years, that is okay. There are remedial steps you can take (tutoring, computer programs, extra school help), but you will not be able—nor should you try—to make a mathematician out of him. It is far better to encourage a child's strengths in other subjects and not emphasize areas of weakness. Most highly selective colleges would much rather see a student who is a genius in one or two areas than someone who is fairly proficient in every area.

You want to encourage your children to work to their full potential and to make sure they have every means, as well as parental support, at their disposal to do their best. This does not mean that they have to get all A's, or stay in honors-level classes if these are really too difficult for their ability level. (I address the issue of tracking in Chapter 11.) You have to be compassionate as a parent and accept your child's limitations. In fact, you want to avoid putting too much pressure on your child's "success." You should celebrate his achievements, but not berate him for his shortcomings.

Keep in mind that some children, especially boys, mature a bit later than others their age. Just because your sixth-, seventh-, or eighth-grader is not getting straight A's does not mean that he won't mature in the first years of high school and hit his stride. If you nag too much, children tend to rebel and decide that they would rather not try at all. Therefore, as a parent, you always have to walk the line between nagging and gently encouraging your child to perform to the best of his ability. While it may be okay to turn up the heat and pressure your child as high school rolls around, it is definitely too early in sixth to eighth grade. It is vitally important that middle school–age kids develop other interests (music, sports, whatever) and be allowed to have a childhood. Play is a key part of growing up.

Books That Every Child Could Use

In addition to setting up an area in the home that is conducive to studying, it is also very important to have some basic reference materials handy at home. I know that with the age of computers and technology much of this material is available on computer, and if you have the money, I would recommend a home computer with a slew of good reference materials plus

Internet access, but I am also cognizant of the fact that not everyone reading this book can afford a fancy computer. With this in mind, let me suggest some books and other resources that are extremely helpful to have at home if you can afford to build up a library of them over time:

- A good high school or collegiate dictionary like Random House or American Heritage
- A good Spanish-English (or whatever language is relevant) dictionary and maybe even a good science dictionary, like the *American Heritage Dictionary of Science* or the *Larousse Dictionary of Science and Technology*
- A good thesaurus for looking up synonyms and antonyms
- A good atlas like *DK's World Atlas* (the maps in *Encarta* and World Book Online are not as detailed and up-to-date for advanced work)
- A nondenominational Bible like the *Oxford Annotated Bible* that has footnotes and explains every passage
- A basic calculator
- An easy-to-follow mythology book, such as *D'Aulairs Illustrated Greek Mythology*, that explains all the Greek and Roman gods, goddesses, and myths
- Educational CD-ROMs for a computer (like Microsoft Encarta) that have a variety of reference materials

As your children get older, you will have to add more to the list, but if your funds are limited, stick to the first two and add the other ones as you can. Even families with limited income can afford these materials if they think of them as holiday and birthday gifts, and when relatives ask, "What does David really need this year for his birthday?" reply that he needs a gift certificate for Barnes & Noble Bookstore, or for time on the Internet, say, using a resource like Amazon.com, more urgently than he needs a new portable CD player. Again, you as a parent are sending a positive message that school is important and that it takes priority over listening to music or playing ice hockey.

Background Music

In theory, I understand the argument that my students make all the time: "But I can concentrate better with my music in the background." I have to disagree. First of all, when they say "in the background," I am suspicious, because the type of music they are listening to is usually not the type of music anyone would consider background music.

Try reading *Catcher in the Rye* with some hip-hop or rap in the background, and you'll see what I mean. Most of my students who say this are definitely not thinking of mellow music like Stan Getz or Bach. Even in the unlikely event that they are, I still disagree because once you are familiar with classical or jazz music, you will want to (and should) sing along and really *listen* to it, not just put it on as background music. Studies have shown that listening to music and reading require the use of two different parts of the brain that can interfere with each other.

If your children love music so much, use it as an incentive for them to finish their work, but not as something to be enjoyed while they are doing their work. Although you may meet a lot of resistance up front, I believe that you are doing your children a big favor in the long run by increasing their concentration spans and making them appreciate and cultivate a love of quiet time. As our society gets more and more fast paced and almost everything in the world can be accessed with a click of a mouse button, it becomes even more important to create a safe haven, a quiet zone, for reflection and serious study. In fact, studies have shown that students learn more efficiently if they speak out loud when they are studying, but music interferes with this process.

Ask any teacher and he or she will tell you that students'

reading comprehension improves dramatically if they are not blasting rock music in the background. One of my colleagues who has taught in schools all over the world insists that the best students he ever had were in Zaire, where they had absolutely no distractions of any kind and were able to study with no interruption.

Of course there are certain types of music (or Muzak) that truly are meant to be background music, so if you find it reasonable, you can experiment. But, as I said, most students are talking about the popular music of their generation, not this kind of music.

Teaching Independence in Routine

As I discussed in the introduction, our goal as parents is to give our children the tools and study skills they need to succeed starting as early as possible, but not to make them dependent on us for the rest of their lives. I have seen too many cases of kids who are so dependent on their parents for everything from laundry to getting up in the morning that they have a terrible time adjusting to college. Needless to say, you want to avoid this kind of dependency at all costs.

You can start teaching this kind of independence even for young middle school children by setting certain parameters and then expecting them to follow them or at least ask you for help if they are having trouble. Let's take the most basic case of getting up in the morning for school. While of course it is possible for you to shake them awake every morning and be their human "snooze" alarm every day from sixth grade to high school, I'm sure you can see that this becomes ridiculous, particularly as they get older. Even when your children are young, it is perfectly reasonable to give them an alarm clock, show them how to set it, discuss how much time they need to get ready in the morning (depending on their routine and how quick they are), and then decide on an appropriate wake-up time.

Though some parents will argue "But Maureen never hears her alarm in the morning and I end up waking her up anyway," one can find plenty of alarm clocks that have a sound so piercing that I doubt any healthy and non–hearing-impaired child could sleep through them. Secondly, if you were to let your child sleep through the alarm one or two days and then he missed school and assignments because of it, he would soon modify his behavior to get up on time. Again, it may be trying for the first few weeks, but keep in mind that our goal is to set lifetime habits. I had hall-mates in college who were constantly sleeping through their morning classes, and their academics suffered greatly because of their lack of accountability. Don't let this happen to your children: As Woody Allen said, "Eighty percent of success is showing up."

The same goes for simple things like children picking out their clothes for the next day (you can require them to spend five minutes the night before to lay out what they want to wear, even if it's a school uniform), having their bookbags packed the night before, having all homework completed before they go to bed (you can check it), and knowing what time they will be picked up at the end of the next day.

Moreover, if you can give your children some household responsibilities from a young age (taking out the trash, washing dishes, setting the table, helping prepare meals, taking care of a younger sibling), you will find that they will become more responsible, less spoiled, more independent, and more self-confident.

One of the brightest and most responsible students in my honors English class is a girl who has several younger brothers and sisters, including a newborn. Her mother relies on her to prepare meals, baby-sit, and keep up with all her work, even though her household responsibilities take up several hours a day. She has learned to budget her time incredibly well. In fact, we are more than halfway through the year and she has yet to miss an assignment or turn one in late. She also has learned to be more caring and compassionate, since she is responsible for the well-being of other family members. If you can even take strides in the direction of increasing your child's responsibilities at home, you will notice a difference in academic performance.

Chapter 3

Nuts and Bolts: Study Skills

How Not to Let Your Child Procrastinate

For both intellectually gifted as well as academically challenged students, the worst enemy they will encounter in their academic lives is procrastination. As parents, your job is to walk the fine line between nagging and enforcing the fact that assignments need to be completed ahead of time, not at the last minute. In my view, there are two major ways you can model children's behavior.

The first way is by example. I am not referring here only to academic affairs. If your children see that you are always putting off your own tasks, whether they be painting the house, washing the car, or shoveling the driveway, they will subconsciously copy your behavior and apply it to their schoolwork.

Imagine your behavior from their point of view: As you leave for work in the morning, you promise your child that you will bake homemade brownies that evening. You come home tired from working all day. Now your child is looking forward to watching you bake and to eating brownies. Suddenly you throw up your arms in despair and say, "Aaagghhh, I don't feeeeeel like baking tonight. Let's just go out for ice cream."

No matter how much your child likes ice cream, he will be disappointed because original expectations were not met, and he will at some level internalize your behavior and even use it as justification for his own behavior. When you, in turn, say to him, "Come on, Mike. Let's finish up your math homework," it's perfectly logical for him to argue, "But I don't feel like it, just like you don't feel like baking—I'm tired!" Now imagine this kind of scene repeated for the entire middle school-year block and you can easily see how children learn to put off things they don't want to do by modeling their behavior on family patterns.

The second way to encourage them to get a jump on work is by using rewards or incentives. Rather than thinking punitively (i.e., you can't go see a movie until you're done with your math homework), you want to dangle a carrot. When your child comes home, sits down in the study space (the one we talked about in the last chapter), and then groans loudly, saying, "I'll never finish my reading—can't I just do it this weekend?" you need to jump in and say, "Come on, it's a great book! Why don't you sit in the living room so you're more comfortable and read half of it now and half before bed? When you get up to Chapter Ten, we'll go outside and shoot some hoops."

This kind of response has several benefits. First, by varying the routine a little and letting your child sit in a comfortable chair, you teach him to associate reading with a positive experience rather than one where he has to suffer by sitting upright. This response also negates his first excuse, which is to complain that he's uncomfortable and can't sit still that long; and it shows your compassion for his feeling pent up and chained to his desk. Second, you've helped him break up a long assignment into two major pieces so that it doesn't seem quite as daunting. You can help him stay ahead by not asking him simply, "Do you have homework tonight?" but rather, "Do you have any *other* homework that's not due tomorrow?"

If you know from looking at his homework notebook that he will be expected to finish *A Separate Peace* by next Friday, you might want to encourage him to read the whole book over the previous weekend so that during the week, when time is short, he can just review the chapters, not actually have to read. Finally, you've provided a positive incentive by offering to take a fun break as a reward for completing the first portion. Young children are particularly motivated by these positive rewards, and they build many positive associations with learning.

To summarize, you can steer your children away from procrastination by using the following techniques:

1. Not nagging them relentlessly
2. Not adopting punitive strategies (If you don't finish, you can't play video games)
3. Keeping them ahead of the game in the first place by using weekends to get ahead on long-term or lengthy assignments
4. Trying to break up their regular study routine in order to make the task seem less monotonous
5. Offering positive rewards such as a game of cards (if you are so inclined), or an unscheduled break

How to Annotate a Book

In my current job, I have had the opportunity to help design the English Department curriculum from grades 6 to 12. One of the biggest benefits of overseeing the middle school and high school curricula is that I can pick what I consider to be the most important lifelong skills (grammar, vocabulary, reading, writing, for example) and make sure they are taught at every level and reinforced in every grade. In my view, the single most important skill for reading comprehension is learning how to annotate a literary work of nonfiction. In fact, once you learn this technique, it is easy to apply to nonfiction reading material in any subject and to some fiction when appropriate.

The key is that you want to teach your children to be active readers, not passive readers. Granted, if you are reading an anthology of the world's funniest jokes for your own enjoyment, it's okay to be a passive reader; after all, no one will quiz you on the material when you finish.

However, if you notice that your children are reading a book for school without appearing to think about it or writing anything down or answering questions, you can be certain that they will miss many important details and will be unable to retain most of the information a day or two later. Annotation involves becoming an active reader, one who is engaged with a text. By reading actively, you bring more of your own participation to the experience of reading, which is what good authors hope for in their readership.

Think of a book as a vast and rich collection of words printed on pages bound together with hundreds of other pages between two covers. If people were to read only passively, then the book's wealth of knowledge and information would all run together in the reader's memory. It takes the mind of an active reader to appreciate the author's careful choice of words and ideas and to remember the information long after the reading is completed.

You can teach active reading to your children well before middle school. At mealtimes, or while riding in the car, or anytime, for that matter, you can tell your child about a wonderful book you yourself are in the midst of reading. You can describe vivid passages, wild travel anecdotes, or remarkable bits of information. Your child will be learning how actively you've read the book, and he'll internalize this impression. Then, when he reads on his own, his mind will be open, receptive, and alert. After years of this type of exposure, your children will find that the process of annotating will come naturally. Again, parents can model the behavior for their children by reading with a pen or pencil in hand and annotating.

What I teach my students is that they want to talk to the text. I teach this to sixth-graders as well as twelfth-graders— the difference is that twelfth-graders are communicating more advanced thoughts. Yet all students can interact with a text at some level, no matter how basic. The first step is that they need to read with a pen in hand. Notice how I did not mention highlighters. I think highlighters tend to be a disservice to the annotation process. In my experience, most students who use them just mindlessly highlight things without giving the highlighted words too much thought. The process is still fairly passive, since they are not actually doing anything with those highlighted lines.

With pen in hand (a bright color like a red or green pen stands out much better from the black text), and only with books the student is allowed to write in, the student wants to do two basic things:

1. In the case of nonfiction, textbooks, biographies, and the like, after reading a page or two, the student writes a quick note at the top of the page just stating key points. An example would be "The three explorers lose sight of land and drift helplessly." By doing this, the student accomplishes two major feats. First, he cannot let his mind wander for ten minutes, only to ask himself later, What was I reading? If he is trained to summarize the main points on each page, he will not let his mind wander nearly as much. Second, it provides easy reference to where everything in the book is located so that when a teacher is leading a discussion and starts talking about a specific detail, the child does not have to sit and listen passively, but rather can turn right to the page the teacher is referring to even before a page reference is given. In effect, it keeps the student a step ahead of his classmates and teachers.

2. Besides just summarizing the major points, the student should then mark up the text by putting an asterisk in the margin next to important events or meaningful details, putting perhaps an exclamation point next to a surprising fact, bracketing a key passage and commenting upon it briefly, putting a plus sign next to particularly informative passages, or using another method of emphasis. Each student need not use the exact same system, but by using sym-

bols to mark important events, it sets them up to do the final step.

If you teach your children to start doing this in sixth grade and you check what they have written, you will be setting them up to be more perceptive and more active readers for life. Annotating not only keeps them focused, but it also forces them to read "acquisitively," gleaning the answers to questions that might be asked later. Although at first the process may seem to slow reading down, in the long run it will make your children better and faster readers who retain more of what they read because they learn to look for specific types of details, for relevant information, and for meaning.

As for reading fictional works (novels, short stories, novellas), the student should experiment to find his own personal method of making only as many notations as he deems useful. It may be more helpful to mark well-written or memorable passages, or where principal characters are introduced, rather than to try to keep track of every detail. In general, fictional works will not need as much notation, but there are of course exceptions to this rule for difficult or complicated works like Dickens' *A Tale of Two Cities* or Conrad's *Heart of Darkness*.

How Do I Help My Child Organize Material for Each Class?

The answer to this dilemma is remarkably simple. Every one of your child's classes should have not only a specific notebook section, but also a simple folder dedicated to that class. Some students like to match a particular color with a particular subject so that if the English folder is green, the English section is marked by a green tab, math with yellow, and so on. Students who do this find that this technique makes it much easier to keep the folders for each subject straight.

Then, within each section of a particular subject, tabs need to be put in for class notes, homework, and annotated notes from the textbook. These three sections should be organized so that the date as well as the chapter or unit being covered are displayed prominently on each page. In order to facilitate your child's ability to keep these sections organized, it's nice to have a sturdy three-hole puncher so that class handouts can be punched and integrated directly into the appropriate section. These handouts or outlines are best placed in the homework section by date.

Let's look at a history notebook for the sake of example. Let's say your child is studying ancient history and is spending about a month on Greece and Rome. In the history three-ring binder, there will be a section labeled "Class notes" in which your child will take notes on what is covered in class. Each page of notes will have "Ancient History: Greece" and the date right on top. Then there will be a section labeled "Homework" where your child will date all the assignments so that once the teacher hands the assignment back, it will make its way chronologically into that section. Finally, there will be a section labeled "Text notes" in which your child will follow the Cornell method (explained shortly).

When the teacher passes out a nicely organized handout on the ancient Greek philosophers, your child needs to date it, three-hole-punch it, write "Ancient Greece" on top, and stick it into the class notes section. Moreover, any tests and quizzes on this unit will go into the color-coded "History: Tests and Quizzes" folder.

In this way, when it's time to study for a unit test or any other cumulative exam, your child can first page chronologically through all the class notes and handouts from the class to review the material the teacher covered. Then he can spend some time reviewing the graded homework assignments. Finally, by way of reinforcing all that has been learned up to that point, he can review his own notes from the text that will summarize and bring into focus much of what was covered in class, not to mention that last step of opening up the "History: Tests and

Quizzes" folder and reviewing all the previous material that was covered on tests by the teacher.

By keeping three or four subsections in each notebook, and by having a three-hole punch handy so that class handouts are never lost (he can always punch them during school hours using a teacher's hole punch), you will find that your child has a much better chance of reviewing material and being able to locate at a moment's notice homework assignments, tests, quizzes, or handouts. The alternative is simply stuffing all of these items together, but that leads to an information overload—too many pieces of paper with no coherent way to organize or systematize, much less assimilate and learn them.

To summarize how to keep a notebook for each subject:

1. Color-code the notebook tab for each subject with the folder for the corresponding subject. The folder for our example should be labeled, "History: Tests and Quizzes."
2. Make three tabs within the subject section.
   (a) class notes and handouts
   (b) homework assignments
   (c) text notes (self-study notes)
3. Try to have a three-hole punch so that all handouts can be punched and then added directly to the correct section by date.
4. Train your children always to put the date and the unit name on every sheet of paper, whether it be a handout or a homework assignment.

Starting with your middle school–age children, you need to train them to not throw away anything a teacher gives them back. Rather, they need to date paper and store them in the appropriate folder. This technique also makes them responsible for and aware of their progress in a class at all times. It's hard for children to argue that they thought they were getting an A if they have a whole folder full of C quizzes.

By creating this folder, when it is time for a unit test or any comprehensive test, your children will be able to locate quickly and review the appropriate material. If you can find stackable paper-holding trays (in an office-supply store), you will aid your children greatly by allowing them to store all their folders neatly.

The biggest stumbling block I find at the high school level is that students either throw out or misplace old exams. In fact, recently I gave my ninth- and tenth-grade English students their comprehensive midterm exams. Although the exam covered all the books, grammar, vocabulary, and writing we studied in the first half of the year, I specifically told them that I would take all the vocabulary antonyms from previous quizzes, all literature questions from previous in-class tests, and all essays from a larger selection of possibilities I had passed out the week before.

I was a bit dismayed to find that most students who did not do well on the exam lost most of their points on the vocabulary section, even though I lifted all those questions from previous tests. In other words, all they had to do was study the last few vocabulary quizzes (I give one a week) to do well. When I looked into the matter, I realized that most of them had thrown out the tests instead of saving them, even though I had specifically told them to save the tests. Don't let this fate befall your children! Get them started at an early age and train them not only to save old tests and quizzes, but to keep them organized from most recent to most ancient so that they can quickly review before any major tests.

One additional benefit of saving returned tests is that, as parents, you will be able to see for yourself how your children are doing in all their subjects by checking these folders on a semi-regular basis. You can also get a sense of your child's teachers by seeing whether they are giving enough feedback on their assignments and enough testing and evaluating. It will keep you much more in touch with how your children are doing academically in each subject area.

How to Outline/Annotate a Textbook Chapter

Now that we have discussed how to annotate a piece of literary nonfiction and, to a lesser extent, fiction, we need to cover how to outline a chapter from a textbook. One problem that becomes immediately evident is that in most public schools, the textbooks are not the student's own to write in! If the student cannot write in the textbook, he can still follow the process I outline by taking notes directly in the subject notebook that corresponds to the textbook. The good news is that the major principles of annotation help us tremendously in this task. In fact, if your child becomes an expert annotator, he probably will not have to generate an outline of each chapter.

Thanks to the fact that 99 percent of all good textbooks have the same organizational format, it is worth getting to know the format so that students learn to work *with* the textbook.

Almost every chapter of any textbook will have a list of objectives of what the student is supposed to learn. The bulk of the chapter, then, is an explanation of the concepts listed in the first section, and the last part is usually a review of what was covered, often with sample questions that address the material in the textbook.

Since it will be nearly impossible to summarize in one sentence all the material on a page, your child needs to look for key words and transitional phrases and then summarize in the margin.

For example, if a math textbook explains that there are three ways to reduce fractions, children need to condense that information into a quick bullet list in the margin by simply writing "(1)," "(2)," "(3)" and the methods right next to them. If a science textbook describes four characteristics of animals and five of plants, your child needs to distill those into list form in the margin. Depending on the density of the textbook (and whether or not the student can write directly in it), it may be easier to outline the chapter on a separate sheet of notebook paper rather than write in the margins.

In terms of summarizing, writing a brief margin note stating what each major paragraph is talking about will keep students focused. Let's suppose they are reading about photosynthesis and the textbook has three paragraphs that describe the process in detail. All they need to do is read the description and then write in the margin next to it, "Description of photosynthesis." This process serves two purposes: (1) It keeps your child focused on the reading, since we all know it is particularly easy for the mind to wander while reading technical material, and (2) it forces them to stop if they have no idea what a paragraph is about and reread it or read it out loud to the point where they can summarize it.

Again, I would interject a note of caution about highlighters, which sometimes turn children into more passive readers who simply drag the highlighter over the text without stopping to think about why what they are reading is important. It is always much more advisable to have them read with pen in hand so they can actively comment and take notes.

The other part of annotating or outlining is that it is very important to jot down questions if something is not absolutely clear. In this way, when a teacher starts class and asks if there are any questions about the reading, your child can immediately raise his hand and say, "Yes, on page 212, I don't understand the difference between Point A and Point B."

A Useful Trick for Guaranteed Academic Success

I have counseled hundreds of students who show up in my office and say, "I just don't get math—I hate it." My next question is always "How well do you know your textbook?" They unfailingly look at me with surprise and say something to the effect of "I barely look at the textbook."

The key to success at all levels is not coming into class unprepared. A student never wants to be in the position of hearing material for the very first time from the teacher. Imagine coming into a math class and sitting there for the whole period while the teacher talks quickly and then gives ten examples of how to factor quadratic equations. Chances are that most students would be so busy trying to follow the explanation and then jotting down notes that they would have trouble picking up the concept.

Here's when the trick comes into play: If the student knows that the teacher will be covering Chapter 4 next week, he should take an hour the night or the weekend before and read through the textbook section. Most textbooks are surprisingly clear in terms of explaining a concept and then giving examples. The student may not understand everything upon a quick first read, but he will have learned at the very least what he does *not* understand.

Imagine then the student arriving in class and actually listening to the teacher explain rather than simply scribbling down notes. Probably 80 percent of the material will now either be review or clarification since the student's brain has already had time to ponder the process.

This prereading step is what distinguishes excellent students from the merely very good. They take the time to preread for every subject, sometimes even jotting down some basic notes so that by the time the teacher teaches, they are oriented and know just how to listen to clear up what they didn't understand and how to review what they learned on their own. I'll be blunt: The math teacher is not really there to teach the student math at all! Most students can learn much of what they need to know right from the textbook. It is far better for students to think of their teachers as a link between the book and their brain, a link who can help clarify and refine what was gleaned from self-study.

The key to mastering material from a textbook is repetition. You need to use the weekends to encourage your child to skim the chapter that the class will cover the following week. This quick reading does not have to be done with a pen in hand. It is really just to get a quick overview of what the class will be covering. Then your child will automatically make active associations when the teacher is explaining a particular topic ("Oh yeah, I remember what a quadratic equation is."). After the teacher has explained parts of a chapter, the child needs to read the chapter actively again, this time in a more formalized way that involves taking notes, annotating, and perhaps outlining.

Finally, before a test or quiz, you should encourage your child to reread the text at least one more time. This last reading will be a much more focused reading, since your child will have already gone through it at least once for an overview, once to outline it, probably another time to do chapter problems or questions, and this last time to memorize information for a test.

This method of reading and rereading is the best training for high school, college, and beyond because it forces students not just to read a textbook, but to study a textbook. By training your children to become active readers, you are helping them gain the skills that will help them for all future schooling. It is important for them to realize at an early age that just reading a chapter once will not help them master it. It is only by rereading and studying and repeating the information over and over again that anyone really comprehends information.

There is an expression that says that once you use a vocabulary word three times correctly, you own it for life. This same principle applies to learning complicated material. If you peruse it before the teacher covers it, then actively read it and annotate and/or outline it, then answer chapter questions and then study your own annotations and outline notes before the test, you will master the material and be able to pinpoint those areas where you might need extra help.

How to Study for Tests

As you might imagine, the key to studying for all tests, no matter what the subject, is repetition. Once your child has mastered the techniques discussed in this chapter for annotating, outlining, and previewing lessons before the teacher covers them, he will be well on his way to mastering the material. Let me break down the process of studying for a test into a few distinct categories.

1. *Gather the material.* If you know your child has a big test coming up on Monday that covers two chapters of social studies, then you should make sure your child understands that he will need three major things: (a) the subject notebook from social studies that contains class notes, text notes, and handouts; (b) the subject folder that contains all previous tests and quizzes; and (c) the textbook itself plus any other notes or outlines that were generated, which should be either in the folder or the notebook.

2. *Sort the material by date to limit the amount of material to be studied.* If the test will cover Chapters 3, 4, and 5, your child needs to review only material from these three chapters and no others. No older homework or tests need to be studied unless the teacher specifically mentions them.

3. *Create a "fact sheet" to review for tests.* I have found that the best way to review for a test is to make a "fact sheet" that differs from the process of taking copious notes. Help your child go back through the textbook so that on a blank piece of paper he can write down the key thoughts and ideas, scattering his ideas all around the page in random physical locations rather than in any consecutive order on the page. It is important that the student not list the ideas in any order. If the text spells out four reasons why George Washington was a great president, the student should write, "George Washington (4)" and nothing else. Once the page

is filled with just a cursory listing of thoughts, ideas, and concepts, have your child close the book and walk around the room with the sheet of paper in hand. The object is to look at the thought or idea and explain it aloud to see if in fact it is stored in the brain. If the student can recall only three of the four facts about Washington, it is clear that more review is needed. The benefit of spreading the words out across the page is that the material need not be covered in order. If the student can reconstruct facts and ideas in a random order, clearly he has learned them.

4. *Begin the process of reviewing in a logical order.* I usually recommend that the child start by rereading the class notes and examples that are contained in the notebook. This should give your child a good idea of what the teacher emphasized in class. If the teacher spent four days reviewing the Battle of Gettysburg, it is a good bet that he will include a big section on that battle in the test. Next, your child should carefully reread the textbook, stopping every few paragraphs to see if he can summarize his own annotations without looking—in other words, memorize them enough to recount the major ideas. Although memorization has become a nasty word in our time, it is still a 100 percent necessary component of studying. Do you know any surgeons who haven't memorized a basic procedure for removing an organ and instead have to rely on a textbook placed next to the patient? Memorization alone is not enough, but memorization of key facts along with comprehension of the concepts will yield the best and most long-lasting knowledge. If the chapter focuses on the causes of the battle, your child should be able to summarize and explain the causes to you. Finally, your child needs to be sure he can answer any questions listed at the end of the textbook or that the teacher posed in class. Many times the teacher will give a study guide or sheet that reviews the material to be included on a test. In this case, the final step

for the child should be to read this sheet at the end and to make sure that he can discuss all the material.

A Test Containing Essay Questions

As students progress to high school level, they will undoubtedly have more writing-oriented tests. Many times teachers will give a choice of essay questions ahead of time. You as parents can help your children get into the practice of outlining their essay so that when they actually sit down during the test, they will have thought the question through completely.

Although you won't want to continue the following process up through your children's entire high school career, it can be both profitably and enjoyably used in the sixth, seventh, and eighth grades: Act as a stand-in for the teacher by testing them on the material yourself. That way, you can coax them toward the answer and think of mnemonic devices or hints that will help them learn the material. Through this process, they can arrive at the answers themselves, but you can lend them your own deductive and reasoning powers to follow the ideas and processes. If the test is something relatively basic such as vocabulary words, be sure they can use them correctly in a sentence they generate. Be sure they can name at least one synonym and one antonym. Be sure they can spell the words accurately.

If the test is on a book, be sure they have both mastered the actual details of plot events and thought about some of the larger thematic issues. If you read over their class notes and annotations, you will find that it is not very hard to test them on the material even if you are not an expert in the subject. You will immediately be able to spot when they are confused, even when you have no idea what the correct answer is.

By volunteering to test your children every so often, you are also affirming that you are interested in helping them, you think their work is relevant, and you are placing a high value on their studies. In fact, you help your children realize that subjects do not exist in a vacuum and that history is connected to English, which is connected to art and music, et cetera. I can't emphasize these points enough. They relate back to our earlier discussion of creating an academic atmosphere at home. In the majority of cases, successful students come from families where an emphasis and importance are placed on academic work above all else. I learned this not just from teaching, but also from the four years I spent working in selective admissions at Dartmouth College.

I had the chance to read thousands of student essays, and what impressed me the most was that those students who truly stood out academically—almost down to a one—had families that placed a strong emphasis on education. I could tell this from the students' essays, which would often be about how their families made sacrifices so that they could devote time to studying, particularly in the case of immigrant families. I can think of literally hundreds of essays that described how parents would take on night jobs and extra work in order that their children, by not being forced to take after-school jobs, could spend the time studying. In Chapter 18 I discuss why in some cases it *is* beneficial for students to have a part-time job. However there *is* a difference between working to augment an education and working to the exclusion of an education. Everything these students' parents ever communicated to them made it clear that they put a higher value on education for getting ahead in life than on any other single factor, whether it be sports, work, or after-school activities.

Remember this obvious fact: Studying and being a serious student take *time* and persistence, not pure genius. When I keep emphasizing repetition, I'm not saying this idly—very few students skim a textbook quickly and then master the material. The adage that genius is 99 percent perspiration and 1 percent inspiration is remarkably astute. Most students I saw who were considering applying to Ivy League schools were those who were both interested in learning and had dedicated a great portion of their lives to learning.

How to Take Class Notes—and Why

In most cases, the question isn't "How do I take notes?" but rather, "Why bother taking notes?" Many bright students mistakenly believe that they already know most of what the teacher is covering and that they need not write everything down. While that thought might get them through years of lower-level course work, there is a big advantage to taking notes, and this is that you can immediately see when reviewing for a test how much class time the teacher has spent on each area. The very process of writing down what a teacher is emphasizing forces the student to pay attention and focus in class.

Of course there are many different systems for taking notes, but I will explain only one, since I think it's the easiest and the most adaptable. The Cornell method of note taking can be used from middle school right up to graduate school and follows three major steps: preparation, during lecture, and after lecture. Lets take a crash course in the Cornell method. The following crash course I'll address directly to the student; therefore parents should urge their children to read it.

Step One: Preparation

The first step is to have your notebook open with loose-leaf paper in the appropriate section for the class. It is preferable to use only the right side of the page and not the back. You will find that if you use the backs it will be much harder to read your notes later and that, furthermore, it is more difficult (for right-handers) to write on the back side of a page that you've flipped over in your loose-leaf binder because it is hard to reach over to that side.

First, draw a vertical line about 2 1/2 inches from the left side of the paper, which effectively divides each piece into a "recall column" on the left and the "note" section on the right. As the teacher talks and writes points on the board, you copy these down on the right side of the paper, leaving the recall column blank.

Step Two: During the Lecture or While Studying Text

As for actually recording notes, try to write as much in simple paragraph form as you can. You don't need to put notes in outline form. In fact, since you won't know the content of the lecture or class ahead of time, it would be almost impossible to outline the material anyway. The object of taking down notes is to use whatever shorthand or abbreviations will help you record the information without slowing you down too much. Although there are many "systems" of shorthand, I have found that just writing quickly and using your own personal shorthand or abbreviations is easier than learning a professional system.

It is not necessary to write down everything the teacher says. What you are trying to do is recapture the main ideas and points. If you are unsure whether something is important enough to include, raise your hand and ask about it. "Do you think we need to memorize all forty-five steps of making ice cream or only the seven you mentioned?" is an example of the kind of questions you would ask.

One final obvious point: Make an effort to write legibly enough that you can read your own writing when you review the notes. If you write in an illegible scrawl, your notes will not be of much use to you.

Step Three: After the Lecture or Text Study

I recommend a daily (or nightly) review of all notes from every class. It will take you only a few minutes for each class, but you will find that this helps you review and retain the information within a twenty-four-hour period of its presentation. It will also help you anticipate the information to be covered in the coming classes.

As you review your notes, draw a box around key words or phrases. For example, if you talked about modernism in your English class and your teacher listed five or so characteristics of the period, you should draw a box around the term *modernism*. Then write the key words and phrases in the "recall column" you have drawn to the left of the main body of notes. After boxing *modernism*, you would write it in the left-hand column so that when you review the notes for a test, you would immediately be able to see where you discuss modernism.

Finally, when you have finished, you will be able to look down the recall column, cover up the right side of the page, and try to remember out loud as many of the key points as you can. If there were five characteristics of modernism and you remembered only four, you need to study them again, cover them up, and try to recite them until you have them in your mind.

The key to this system is not waiting until the end of the marking period or quarter to review your notes. It is a million times harder to reread a whole semester's worth of notes than to spend a few minutes each night reviewing and studying the day's material before going on to new material.

More than any other study habit, constant review of notes will lead to better retention of information, more organized notebook keeping (since you are constantly anticipating the material to come), and higher grades. Note taking becomes the most important study skill to master.

Chapter 4

The Homework Dilemma: How Much Help Is Too Much? How Much Homework Is Too Much?

Getting Set Up

We have already covered how to help your children keep track of their homework and how to make sure they keep a homework notebook with all daily assignments. I think it's fair when your children are in middle school to oversee how they set themselves up for doing their homework and to review the day's assignments with them before they begin.

If you need to, remind your child to put all the textbooks and notebooks he will need out on his worktable, and then have him give you a rundown of what he has to do. Don't accept "But I don't have anything" as an answer. If, for example, your child tells you that he has nothing to do for language arts class, you might ask when he needs to finish the book the class is reading. It is always a good idea to get ahead so that school nights can be spent reviewing or rereading, not reading for the first time. Remember, repetition is the key to success.

How Much Parental Help Is Too Much?

I have seen too many parents actually do their children's homework for them. Although it sounds obvious, let me state the

point boldly: You will *not* help your children in the long run
if you do their homework for them. My uncle used to do all
my mother's math homework when they were growing up. Not
only did she fail miserably in math class, to this day she needs
a calculator to do simple tasks such as leaving a 15 percent tip
at a restaurant. Your goal as parents is to facilitate the completion of homework, never to complete it for them.

The best ways you can help are ways we have already discussed: Set up an environment conducive to studying, have children review with you what they have to do, make sure they
have all reference materials they need, make sure they eat some
healthy food so they have the brainpower to think, and show
interest in what they are doing. You do not want to substitute
your effort for theirs—ever. Feel free to refer your children to
the helpful homework Web sites listed in Appendix A before
you rush to their aid.

What exactly is your role as a parent? In a nutshell, you can
explain any material they are having trouble with, review material for a test or help them memorize something, give examples of problems so that they can learn a methodology, suggest
places to look up answers, but do not do it for them. In addition, stress the relevance of what they are learning to their
everyday life, even if it's something as simple as integrating
what they are learning in history class to what is on the evening
news.

Let's say you are a math whiz and have no trouble completing your daughter's algebra homework. Let's walk through
an example of how to help with a specific homework problem
without doing it for her.

Your daughter is having trouble figuring out how to solve
for x in a simple equation like $2x + 5 = 11$. You need to take
the time to explain in smaller steps how to solve this one equation, and then watch her to see if she can apply the method to
the other problems. Of course, explaining each step to your
child takes much more time than merely doing the problem for
your child, yet it is the best and only way.

On a piece of scrap paper, write down the problem and explain that you first need to get the part with the x all by itself. How to do this? Well, you need to add -5 to the left side of the equation. But if you do something to one side of an equation, you must do the same thing to the other side to keep the value the same. Stop for a second to see if she understands what you have just said. Now write it out as such, showing the step: $2x + 5\ \mathbf{-5} = 11 + \mathbf{-5}$. Notice the bold-faced numbers, which show that we added -5 to each side.

Now follow through. The left side now has only $2x$, while $11 - 5$ on the right side leaves us with 6. Once we have isolated the x term, we need to get rid of the coefficient. When we are dealing with these numbers, it is necessary to multiply by a fraction to get rid of the 2. The only way to get rid of the 2 is to multiply it by its inverse, which is $1/2$. Make sure she understands that this works for all numbers. With $5x$, you'd multiply by $1/5$, with $10x$, you'd multiply by $1/10$ since when you cross-multiply, it always leaves you with $1x$ which is the same as x, what we are solving for.

Once again, if you do something to one side of the equation, you must do the same thing to the other. Therefore, $(1/2)\ 2x = 6\ (1/2)$. After we cross-multiply, we get $x = 3$. Once she has followed all these steps, make sure she understands the concept and that you can check the answer by plugging the number 3 right back into the original equation. Be sure to follow through on this last step even if the teacher does not require it. Now we can see that $2(3) + 5 = 11$. Sure enough, $6 + 5 = 11$, $11 = 11$. Therefore, we are now positive that the answer is indeed 3.

By modeling one full problem like this and breaking it down into steps, you have not done the assignment for your child. You have shown her in more detail how to solve for an entire system of equations. Now your job is to let her try the next few problems and follow the steps. If she leaves something out, give a gentle reminder like "Now if you add something to one side of the equation, you must add the same thing to the other side so you don't change the value."

The cardinal rule is, *Keep your patience!* If you start yelling, or insulting children, their brains will turn off or they will become so angry that they turn against you and resist you and your help. The object is to keep them focused on the problem. It also helps if you can give them some reason why this material will be useful to them outside of school. In the case of algebra, you might point out that these same steps can be used to solve practical problems like how long it will take you to get to your grandmother's house if you drive sixty miles per hour and you live forty-five miles away. In the case of a foreign language, you might point out that conjugating verbs actually will help your children to communicate in foreign countries.

Your attitude is of paramount importance. If you relay to your child that you don't think the homework is important or relevant, he will have an easy argument as to why he shouldn't do it at all.

As I said before, share your knowledge and enthusiasm about a particular field with your children. If they are reading *To Kill a Mockingbird*, discuss the issues of the case with them in terms they understand. If they are studying Spanish, show them pictures from a Spanish-speaking country like Spain or Mexico and narrate any past experiences you may have had there. If they are studying World War I, you might want to tie in nightly news coverage of a current war with the causes of World War I. In these small ways, you inculcate in your children a love of learning because you show not only that you care, but also that the material they are learning is pertinent to everyday life.

A good modern-day example of an opportunity to make school subject matter relevant is the Clinton impeachment process. If your son was studying social studies at the time and learning about concepts such as Congress and the House and Senate, you could open any paper and read to him the daily proceedings, which explained in much greater detail than a middle school class the entire process and how one could impeach a president. I daresay that most children who lived through the proceedings acquired a full-fledged knowledge of how our government works to a greater extent than they ever could have in a class.

If your child has to write an essay that involves library research, take her to the library, show her how to find the information, help her take notes, but do not do it for her! You can even make it more interesting by taking her favorite hobby first and showing her how to research more information on that topic. In this way, children will learn that they can use research skills for their own personal interests as well as for school interests. If they get used to depending on you, you are helping them only in the short run.

Howard Gardner, creator of the theory of multiple intelligences and professor at the Harvard Graduate School of Education, puts it well when he emphasizes that our job as parents is to amplify what our children learn in school:

> Let's say instead that homework were seen not as an intrusion but rather as a daily occasion where major tasks and opportunities of growing up could be worked through. . . . Homework can amplify what one already values as a parent or child. . . . Homework seems less problematic in Asian societies because families and schools are already in accord on the need for home study. Indeed, when Asians move to America, parents often purchase their own copies of textbooks so they can learn along with their children.

I like his example of Asian parents because it highlights what I always try to emphasize: The more credence you give to your children's work, the more they will understand the value of learning and of doing homework. You don't find many Asian parents in the United States who complain that teachers assign too much work. In fact, in many cases these parents assign their children extra problems, particularly in math, if they feel the teacher is not covering enough material. Keep in mind that your children are really competing in a worldwide competition, not just a national competition, particularly with the increase of technology (that connects us instantly to anywhere in the world), international business, and international education programs such as the International Baccalaureate.

The entire goal of helping your children is to teach them enough about the process of doing homework and fact-finding that they will be able to work completely independently and will know when to ask for help.

Acknowledging Parental Help

In the case where you really did help your child with a specific task (perhaps you helped her footnote a paper even though she hadn't learned how to in class), I would recommend writing a note to the teacher explaining exactly how you helped your child. Coming from the teaching side as I do, I can tell you that I'd much rather know exactly how a parent helped out with an assignment than have to sit there questioning how much of the student's work is his own. You don't want to do this regularly, but in the few cases where you do contribute either by teaching a new mathematical method of solving a problem or showing your child a technique he hasn't learned, be honest and let the teacher know in writing what role you have had.

This honesty will go a long way in creating a good working relationship with a teacher and also in sharing the lesson with your children that it is not right to take credit for work if they did not do it all themselves.

How Can You Tell if Your Child Studies Too Much or Too Little?

A recent *Time* magazine cover story ("Too Much Homework: How It's Hurting Our Kids, and What Parents Should Do About It," by Romesh Ratnesar, January 25, 1999, pp. 56–62) argues that too many elementary and middle school students find themselves having to do three to five hours of homework a night, which adds to their stress level and makes them hate learning.

> The homework crunch is heard loudest in the country's better middle-class school districts, where parents push their kids hard and demand that teachers deliver enough academic rigor to get students into top secondary schools and colleges. Now there's a blow back: the sheer quantity of nightly homework and the difficulty of the assignments can turn ordinary weeknights into four-hour-library-research excursions, leave kids in tears and parents with migraines, and generally transform the placid refuge of home life into a tense war zone.

In my opinion, this kind of homework load is too much— the key should be quality, not quantity. Good teachers assign enough work so that the student has time to reflect on what he learned in school and has the chance to apply it to a nightly assignment. In the best of cases, teachers assign enough work to reinforce what was learned, allow reflection and assimilation of material, and drill home important models so that a student commits them to memory. Unfortunately, some teachers do assign busywork. Clearly, in the example cited above, I would disagree with giving such a copious amount of homework, particularly if it seemed that most of it was busywork and not targeted enough to the material actually covered in class.

Needless to say, there is the opposite extreme of not having enough homework to have any hope of mastering the material. As you can imagine, there is a fairly direct link between income level and quality and quantity of homework. A case in point are inner-city schools. As the *Time* article points out, "In contrast to their overburdened counterparts in private and suburban schools, students in Boston's 11 public district high schools give homework such a low priority that many no longer bother to carry a backpack. Frustrated teachers say often only a handful of students turn in homework, making it nearly impossible to discuss course material."

I tend to err on the side of assigning a little too much work rather than not enough, since I believe that, compared to other societies, we still work less overall and do much worse on all national tests in math and science and language than many foreign students. During the four years I was an assistant admissions director at Dartmouth College, I had the opportunity to read all the applications from the People's Republic of China. The competition to get into an Ivy League school is tremendous from the PRC because 150 to 200 students apply, but since they all need a full financial aid package, we would accept at most three students a year. As you would guess, these students study English for hours upon hours to be competitive in an international pool of applicants.

What impressed me the most was the Chinese students' scores on the GRE (Graduate Record Exam), which is the graduate-school equivalent of the SAT and the test they had to take since the SAT was not offered in the PRC. Even though they were taking a more advanced exam than the SAT, the best students still scored in the 700 to 800 range on the verbal section (they almost always scored 750 to 800 on the math and analytical section) because they studied vocabulary and read books in English to prepare. In effect, they scored better than the majority of educated American students who have spoken English all their lives simply because they dedicated themselves to studying and learning the material; they knew their future depended on it.

In the *Time* article, the author cites Harold Stevenson and James Stigler's book *The Learning Gap* to show that Japanese and Chinese elementary school students spend much more time on homework than do American children. "A first-grader in Taipei does seven times as much homework as a first-grader in Minneapolis—and scores higher on tests of knowledge and skills." He then goes on to say that "American parents should worry less about the precise number of minutes their students devote to homework and more about the uneven and poorly conceived way in which it is assigned." Shouldn't American students be worried that applications from foreign students to American universities are expanding exponentially? If American students waste their opportunities for admission, their spaces may go to more-prepared foreign students who are ready for the challenge.

As I mentioned earlier, I totally agree that busywork should be avoided. Busywork or major projects (multimedia time lines, collages, complicated family trees) that parents have to end up doing do not help to prepare our children for college. All they really do is cause stress for parents and students alike and stifle a love of learning at the same time. A healthy balance must be achieved so that students are assigned enough to teach them the organizational and study skills they will need to succeed without pushing them to becoming sleep-deprived in seventh grade.

One way to let teachers know how long it takes your child to do homework is to have your child write at the bottom of the math worksheet, or whatever the assignment was, how many minutes the assignment took. I know many teachers who don't realize that the assignment they thought would take forty-five minutes took most students two hours. If your child makes it a habit to write down the time an assignment took, teachers can have constant feedback without your having to march into school to complain. In the case of a student who is truly a whiz in the subject, it's probably better to leave this out since a teacher may interpret taking a short amount of time to do homework as a lack of effort, when the truth is that the student simply was able to complete the assignment quickly because of high ability.

In extreme cases where you and other parents have gotten together and feel that the homework load is unreasonable, you can put together a committee to make positive suggestions, as many public districts have done. They usually suggest that teachers assign work that is "meaningful and purposeful" and limit the load by grade level, so for sixth grade the limit might be thirty minutes per subject per night. As a general rule, though, unless the load is truly unreasonable, I would probably just try to support your children and not attack teachers. You don't want to teach your children the lesson that you can bail them out of any situation if the going gets tough.

The point is that while homework can get overwhelming every once in a while, it's a bad thing only if your child is overwhelmed on a daily basis. Again, you should always encourage your children to use a weekend day to help themselves get ahead for the week, particularly in subjects such as English that require a lot of reading—a task that is always easier to do on the weekend when a child is rested than during the week when the child might have piano lessons, karate, and dance lessons in addition to regular homework.

As a rough guideline, in sixth to eighth grade, it's reasonable to expect a total load of two to four hours a night, but not more than that unless there is some kind of special project. At the school where I currently teach, we limit teachers to thirty minutes per night per subject (as a guideline) at the middle school level and forty-five to sixty minutes per subject per night at the high school level. If your sixth-grader has five hours of homework a night, either he has a learning problem of some sort (see Chapter 12, "Learning Disabilities") or something is out of whack in your school district. You need to talk to other parents to find out if the homework takes their children the same amount of time, or whether your child is struggling because of his own individual problems. If, after speaking to other parents, you realize that it takes your child much longer to complete his nightly homework than it does other children, you may want to consider a full battery of tests for learning disabilities and processing problems. I will cover this later.

In short, be sensitive to your child's needs, monitor the homework and evaluate for yourself whether it seems reasonable, and provide constant positive feedback and guidance without actually doing the work for him.

Other Resources for Homework Besides Tutoring

In addition to the basic reference books that I recommended earlier, one homework resource that is expensive but worth the money is offered by an innovative company called the Teaching Company: Great Courses on Tape (1-800-832-2412). I could easily recommend all the college-level courses geared toward parents or very advanced high school students, but they also have a fantastic high school section with courses in math, science, and English. One teacher I recommend personally is Dr. Murray Seigal, Ph.D., who teaches pre-algebra (basic math) and Algebra II, which combines Algebra I and II. Though you may have to lay out $50 to $150 up front, it will still end up being cheaper than hiring a tutor and is, in many cases, every bit as good.

Should I Limit My Child's Use of Internet Chat Rooms, Web Surfing, TV, Computer Games, and Phone Conversations?

In a word, yes. I remember back in my freshman year of college when we had a brand-new simultaneous chat room that functioned on the campus called "xyz." It was very novel because you could participate in an anonymous conversation over the computer with a group of people twenty-four hours a day. You got to know people through their code names, and you had the ability to reinvent your persona any day of the week. The only problem was that there was a huge rash of academic failure because large groups of students got addicted to the game and stopped going to class and doing work. Several of my classmates failed out of college the first couple semesters.

While there are certainly positive ways to use the Internet (chat rooms are not the first one I'd list) for research or news, it should never interfere with homework time. If you follow the schedule I set forth in Chapter 1, these diversions are not an option until all homework is not only done, but also done to your standards. Hastily scribbling off a math homework problem rather than showing all the steps and writing it out neatly just doesn't cut it.

As a parent, you have to take a firm stand. It's not healthy for students to watch TV or to sit in front of a computer monitor for hours a day.

Just recently during a parent conference at our school, a desperate mother said to us, "My son spends six hours a night on the computer and there's nothing I can do about it." Of course there is! You don't have to pay the bill for his America Online account, you don't even have to allow him to use the computer—he's your son! She was extremely relieved to hear us say that it was okay to pull the plug.

Of course on occasion it's fine for students to veg out and take a complete break, but you can be sure that if they spend hours a night on the computer, then something is not right; unless of course they are teaching themselves programming languages or learning to speak Chinese through an educational program. I think, though, you'll find that usually they are simply surfing the Net, entering chat rooms, and just fooling around. Pull the plug! Suggest that your children read books instead, or play outside, or do anything else that is more ac-

tive than staring at the TV. Remember, for every hour of reading a child does, there is an enormous payback down the road
in terms of everything from increased attention span to a higher
verbal SAT score.

Chapter 5

Egghead Tips for Success: Homework Shortcuts for Students from Successful Students

Now that we have covered how to study and take notes, I thought it would be helpful to hear directly from some successful students regarding shortcuts and tips for homework and studying for tests. Although they all know how to take notes and study as I have described in previous chapters, the best students know when it is appropriate to take shortcuts and when it is better to do things the long way. I have kept their advice in their own words, addressed directly to the student who is looking for a more expeditious way to accomplish common tasks:

- Never procrastinate. Procrastination leads to rushing, and rushing leads to missing information.
- Plan to finish certain assignments ahead of time because it will reduce much of the stress you face.
- Go to class and always pay attention. You would be surprised how much you will retain just by being present and listening, even if you never crack open a book. Ninety percent of the material for tests and quizzes will have been covered in class.
- Don't try to write down everything the teacher says in class. Just concentrate on a few key words and phrases that will remind you of what was being discussed.

- Date all material that a teacher hands back and date all your notes. That way when it comes time for a big test, you can group all the material covered in a particular time period together.
- Study with another person in your class who is on a similar academic wavelength. That way, you can compare notes and review material together.
- Class participation is a key to becoming a good student. Have confidence in your own ability.
- If you don't understand something, speak up in class! Ask the teacher to explain it again. If you still don't get it, see the teacher after class or after school. If the teacher starts to explain it again the same way, remind her that you didn't understand it the first time and maybe she could try an alternate explanation. While it is not a teacher's job to be a mind reader and to figure out when you don't understand something, it is a teacher's job to be able to explain material three or four different ways. If you still don't get it after four explanations, consider a tutor.
- If you have free time in school (i.e., study halls, lunch) use the time wisely—it could mean less homework in the long run.
- During lectures always take notes no matter how well you think you know the material—it reinforces the material and reminds you what the teacher went over in class.
- Don't let your extracurricular activities take priority over your academics.
- Always spell-check and proofread carefully anything you hand in for grading—teachers are turned off by careless errors.
- When reading full chapters for a test, never read word for word the first time. Start from the beginning and skim the chapter, reading the first lines of paragraphs and some information here and there. Then read the chapter again. The first time will give you an overview of the chapter and the second time will give you the rest of the information.

- Read chapters ahead of time. Nothing is ever wrong with learning what you will need for class beforehand: (1) You'll be able to answer questions in class, and (2) it makes you look good in front of your teachers.
- Make outlines, even if your teacher does not require them, especially for long, tedious textbooks like history and science. These outlines will help you organize material for tests.
- Buy *Cliffs Notes* or other helpful reading aides such as the *Bloom's Notes on Literature* or the *Norton Critical Editions*. Though they never take the place of reading a book, they provide lots of useful background and plot information.
- In science and math textbooks, there are always boldfaced and italicized words. When reading, always skip forward to read these words. They will be the focus of tests. Write them all down and let them serve as your study guide (and of course go back and read the rest of the words).
- When reading novels, annotate and fold pages. During discussions and studying for tests, you will always need to remember where something is. If you know the chapter well, you'll be able to find any important scene quickly.
- In history textbooks, a major key word that helps you study for a test is *reason* (i.e., the reason for the Catholic Reformation). Pay close attention to the material that follows the word *reason*.
- Study with several other people who are at about your level. As work gets more reading oriented, study groups can help you understand the material and get the last few details for an exam.
- Oftentimes in math, it's better just to do three or four problems and then skip one when you know the principle at work—otherwise, it's busywork.
- If you forgot about a test or quiz that is given that day, don't panic! It's only one test. Keep a positive frame of mind, which will automatically increase your score. Tell yourself, "I know this information like the back of my hand." If you keep your

brain free of panicky thoughts, you will do much better. Half the game is mental.

- If you forgot to study, before the test, try to quiz someone in your class who has studied to reinforce some of the major points. One day they'll return the favor.

- Use a planner. If you don't, someday you'll forget an assignment and the extra few points can mean a higher final grade.

- Don't ask competent teachers for extra credit in high school. It doesn't happen. Instead, if you're failing a class and are already getting extra help, do something on your own and turn it in. Even if the teacher doesn't grade it, he'll be impressed at your effort, and that helps with subjective grading.

- Most people have a couple of hours of peak productivity. Figure out when yours are and save them for creative writing and studying for tests. The rest of the day, do little, easy assignments and take frequent breaks; but don't stall. Finishing your homework means you can stall the rest of the night.

- Looking ahead to high school, make sure you enjoy learning about the subjects you are taking. If you are genuinely interested in what you are learning, reading suddenly stops sounding like a chore.

- If you take a bus to school, use the time to read schoolbooks and sleep. Listening to music might be more fun, but you only have so much free time. Chances are if you were home or out with friends, you might have better things to do.

- If you do nothing else, study for tests. Never assume you'll do poorly; many tests can be aced with an hour's solid study even if you don't understand some concepts. However, don't study for one class during a different class because you won't learn anything from either class.

- Buy a leading textbook *not* being used at your school. Use this text to validate or revise your list of most important concepts and vocabulary for each section. You may even get a "zinger" for class that no one knows, sometimes not even the teacher!

- Again, looking ahead to high school, for the SAT II and AP exams: Your goal is to "own" the exam. Start early and practice every test that the College Board releases. Reviewing mistakes will let you pinpoint your "crash review" program.
- Review in detail the contents of a pocket dictionary (50,000 words). Find the 3,000 to 5,000 words you don't know. If you do twenty words per week for three years of high school, you will be a "walking dictionary" and be closer to that 800 verbal score!

Chapter 6

Keeping Your Child's Guidance Counselor in the Loop as a Key Resource: Creating a Course of Studies

The Seventh-Grader's Map to Courses in Grades 8–12

It doesn't occur to most parents to take some of the burden off their shoulders by using the school's own resources. In the case of young middle school children, it is very important to try to sit down with a guidance counselor and map out a tentative long-range course plan. Many students wait until halfway through high school before they examine their course options, but by this time it can be too late if they have specific career goals. For example, a student who wanted to enter a career related to math and computer science would want to make sure that a tentative course plan included math up to at least pre-calculus or AP calculus by the end of high school.

Also, if your child is starting behind for some reason, you can develop a long-range plan to play catch-up (i.e., summer school, or after-school enrichment programs) so that he can have a full range of options.

Make an appointment with your child's guidance counselor (your child should definitely be at this meeting!) and bring along a chart similar to the one on the next page.

	7th Grade	8th Grade	9th Grade	10th grade
English				
Math				
History/S.S.				
Science				
Foreign Lang.				
Other				

Have your child explain some of his career goals and ideas; they can be creative as long as the child realizes that entering even a fanciful field like being an astronaut will require a very specific course of study.

You'll want to emphasize to your child that this kind of long-range planning can be fun—pretend you are organizing a trip to Europe or Africa. Just as with arranging a trip, all will go much more smoothly in life if there is a long-range plan. Having the guidance counselor go through these options with you and your child will force you to consider certain choices. If your child loves languages, for example, how will he be able to schedule in a second language while still fulfilling the high school's fine arts requirement? Making the chart will also force you to plan ahead for any special credit requirements that the high school and middle school might have that you didn't know about (mandatory gym, arts courses, et cetera).

Ask for a copy of the high school course-planning guide (all high schools should have one) and examine sample copies of student schedules at the high school level even if your child is only a middle-schooler. That way, your child has something to model his course selection on.

As a side benefit, if your child has to think about long-range plans, he will be more motivated along the way. When he suddenly realizes that he needs to reach AP calculus in order to be an investment banker, he will take his seventh-grade math class more seriously, since he can see the whole sequence laid out before him. This chart can be revisited year after year, but you want at least to get the ball rolling early on and to let the guidance counselor know that you are involved and interested in your child's academic life.

There are many questions you should ask your middle-schooler's guidance counselor. The following is a general list, which can be added to so that when you make an appointment you will have a clear agenda.

1. What basic academic courses are recommended for college-bound students?
2. What are the graduation requirements for middle school and high school? (Particularly non-academic ones, like fine arts, drama, gym, and the like.)
3. What is the homework difference in honors classes versus non-honors classes?
4. What are the criteria for being accepted into advanced classes?
5. What activities can students do at home or during summer break to prepare for college?
6. Are there special tutoring services offered by the school?
7. Does the school offer in-house test preparation for the SAT Is and SAT IIs?
8. What colleges did students from previous classes attend?
9. What organizations are responsible for accrediting the middle school and high school?
10. How should teachers be contacted if a student needs extra help?
11. What college resources does the school provide and in what grade does college counseling start? (In many fine schools, the process starts in eighth or ninth grade, not twelfth!)

Other Ways to Utilize Your Guidance Counselor

Your child's guidance counselor can be useful in other aspects of your child's middle school academic progress. In a later chapter we discuss learning disabilities and other problems that can interfere with learning. If for any reason you feel that your child is not working up to his potential, you should make an appointment with the guidance counselor, who can review standardized test scores with you and give a professional opinion as to what the options are.

A trained guidance counselor should be able to interpret IQ scores and any other test scores in your child's file and hold these scores next to his actual achievement. Often the guidance counselor will notice a learning problem well before it is officially diagnosed.

In addition, your guidance counselor should be able to help you and your child as far as tracking is concerned. If you feel that your child is placed either too high or too low for his ability level, ask the guidance counselor what he recommends. He should be able to write out for you on the above chart several different course projections, depending upon whether your child follows an honors track, a regular track, or a modified track. If you make it a point to meet with the guidance counselor at least once every academic year, you will be able to update this course projection based on your child's actual achievement versus his projected achievement.

Finally, you should ask the guidance counselor to get involved with teacher conflicts. No matter how easygoing your child is, it is probable that at some point he will either despise a certain teacher or feel that he is unable to learn with that teacher. The guidance counselor can serve as an intermediary between you and your child and the teacher in question and is often able to resolve a conflict before it escalates.

Be sure to get your child involved in the academic planning process so that he will have a stake in the outcome. Use your school's guidance counselor as an important resource to help you both plan for the future and to resolve any conflicts that come up during the year.

Chapter 7

What Is Plagiarism and How Can It Be Avoided?

Many colleges (and a good number of high schools) automatically expel a student who plagiarizes. Sadly, I would bet that many of those students never really learned exactly what plagiarism was when they were in middle and high school. Remember, ignorance of the law is no defense— all students need to know exactly what constitutes plagiarism so they never even come close to committing this potentially disastrous mistake. All schools have different punishments for plagiarism and different interpretations of the basic premise, but the offense of plagiarism itself is fairly standard across the country.

What exactly is plagiarism, anyway? By definition, plagiarism is: *The appropriation or imitation of the language, ideas, and thoughts of another author, and representation of them as one's original work* (from the Latin plagiarius, kidnapper).

Stated simply, plagiarism is using someone else's words or ideas as if they were your own, or taking credit for someone else's work.

The most interesting observation to make is that *intent* is not part of the definition of plagiarism. In other words, whether a student plagiarizes on purpose or because he didn't understand what he was doing is irrelevant! Just as when the policeman says you were going seventy miles an hour in a thirty-mile-an-hour zone, it doesn't matter if you say you didn't realize the speed limit was only thirty or whether you explain why you were speeding on purpose—the cop doesn't care! The sentence for those who were speeding on purpose is no stiffer than for those who did it entirely by accident.

Therefore, it is vital to understand how to avoid plagiarism and when it is necessary to cite information. The bottom line is that if a student obtains information or ideas from an outside source, that source *must* be acknowledged. The most important rule to follow is that any direct quotation must be placed in quotation marks, and the source immediately cited.[1]

Different Types of Plagiarism

There are three major ways a student can plagiarize, so you and your child need to examine all three in some detail:

1. *Plagiarism by unacknowledged verbatim quotations.* For example, if a student uses *Cliffs Notes* to write a paper and lifts specific phrases and quotes from them ("the real conflagrations of battle") without mentioning that the *Cliffs Notes* had been consulted, he would be guilty of plagiarism by using an exact, or verbatim, quote. Likewise, if a student lifts three sentences straight out of *Time* magazine but neglects to mention that a columnist wrote the sentences, he is guilty of using exact or verbatim quotes. It is perfectly okay to write "Joe Smith in his May 4 *Time* magazine article says, . . ." because the quote is acknowledged as someone else's words.

2. *Plagiarism by mosaic, or mixing paraphrase and unacknowledged quotation.* Even if the student completely rewords a summary from the *Cliffs Notes* yet accidentally repeats a

---

[1] Dartmouth College, *Student Handbook* (Hanover, 1997), p. 147. Much of the material in this chapter is modelled on this handbook and some of the examples are taken directly from it. But since I acknowledge the liberal borrowing, it is *not* plagiarism.

phrase without quoting it and citing it, he is guilty of plagiarism. This would be considered mixing a direct quote with a paraphrased summary that was done by someone else. The most important thing to keep in mind is that if your child is going to try to paraphrase someone else's ideas, be sure that he uses footnotes or gives credit in parentheses to the author of those ideas. Be aware that it is very easy to slip in a phrase or two from a source even if one is trying one's best to paraphrase it.

That rule brings up this next point: It is most prudent that your child avoid paraphrasing altogether when doing research papers or essay writing. All he is really doing is taking someone else's thoughts and trying to change the words around so they sound like his own. It is far better for a student to quote a source directly and then give credit than to try to paraphrase it himself, since paraphrasing just weakens the rhetorical effect of an essay.

3. *Plagiarism by unacknowledged paraphrase and/or use of ideas.* This last category is very similar to the previous one, except that it highlights the fact that it is plagiarism to borrow even someone else's *ideas.* For example, if a student reads about Einstein's theory of relativity and then writes, "I think that time probably is relative depending on the speed an object travels because I watched a train go by and it makes sense," it is pretty clear that he is liberally borrowing from Einstein one of his most famous ideas.

Why Should Sources Be Acknowledged, Anyway?

Now that we know what constitutes plagiarism, let's look at why it is important to acknowledge through citations where ideas and quotes come from.

First, citations reflect the careful and thorough work that was put into locating sources for research. Why not get credit for work that was actually done? If your child actually checked out ten library books and found seven magazine articles, why should she not take credit for finding good sources and doing good research?

Second, citations are a courtesy to the reader, who may share the writer's interest in a particular area of scholarship. They help readers understand the context of the argument as well as help locate the work within other conversations on the writer's topic. An avid reader might want to chase down several more in-depth articles on a subject by looking up the materials listed in the footnotes. Furthermore, citations allow the writer to acknowledge those authors who made possible particular aspects of the work. Why not give credit where credit is due? Finally, citations draw attention to the originality and legitimacy of the writer's own ideas. The reader might suspect that a really interesting idea was copied anyway, but if this same reader can see that the writer has given a nod to others with different ideas, the true original idea stands strong against the backdrop of others' ideas.

When Should Your Child Cite Sources?

1. *Cite sources for all verbatim (that is, "exact word") quotations of two or more consecutive words.* Readers expect to know the original source of any quotation, whether for the purpose of checking its accuracy or using it in their own work. Your child must place the words, or even one word, in quotation marks to make it very clear which word or words he is quoting.

Example: My teacher always mentioned the famous lines of his favorite Edgar Allan Poe poem, "Quoth the raven, nevermore."

Example: I have always believed Benjamin Disraeli's thoughts on the matter: "It is better to be critical than correct."

Your child needs to provide a footnote after each of the above quotes!

2. *Your child must cite sources for ideas or information that could be regarded as common knowledge but that (1) your child did not possess before and (2) your child thinks his reader*

might still find unfamiliar. When in doubt, just footnote it anyway. Some ideas that would not have to be footnoted: the Oedipus complex (as long as the writer is not taking credit for inventing it), Watergate, the theory of relativity, the Lewinsky affair, the structure of water as H_2O, the fact that Jane Austen wrote *Pride and Prejudice.*

Your child does need to cite specific sources for information that he judges his readers might find unfamiliar, for example that *Pride and Prejudice,* unlike many English novels written in the years following the French Revolution, endorses pleasure and happiness;[2] or that Darwin seems to have been an undistinguished student at Edinburgh.[3]

3. *Your child must cite sources from which he paraphrases or summarizes facts or ideas.* As we have said, your child should avoid paraphrasing as much as possible, since it weakens the rhetorical effect of his work.

4. *Your child must cite sources that add relevant information to the particular topic or argument of his work.* This is more for when he is writing in a very in-depth way on a topic (like a thesis or research paper) and wants to help his reader pursue a related interest.[4]

5. *Your child must cite sources for materials that he might not normally consider "texts" because they are not written.* Some examples would be Web pages, statistical tables, electronic databases, lectures, TV shows, and movies.

I will not go into specific examples of footnoting format (footnotes appear at the bottom or "foot" of each page, while endnotes appear at the end of the paper), since every teacher has the right to request a certain system. The most popular format nowadays is usually the MLA (Modern Language Association) format.

---

[2]Claudia L. Johnson, *Jane Austen: Women, Politics, and the Novel* (Chicago: University of Chicago Press, 1988), p. 78.

[3]Adrian Desmond and James Moore, *Darwin* (London: Joseph, 1991), p. 27.

[4]For a delightful history of citation practices, see Grafton. (This, by the way, is a supplementary citation and one that is cited in the Dartmouth handbook. Again, I didn't want to plagiarize!)

Chapter 8

Computers: Are They Indispensable for Success?

Certainly no one can dispute that our children need to develop computer skills in order to survive in our society. Most universities expect children to be comfortable taking notes on laptops, doing research on the Internet, and being able to communicate by E-mail.

However, I tend to err on the more conservative (some would say Neanderthal) side of trying to understand that while technology is a great thing, it's not a panacea. In a recent debate in *Time* magazine, David Gelernter, a computer-science professor at Yale, took on Al Gore regarding the issue of whether all schools should be wired to the Internet in order to keep American students on the cutting edge of technology. While Gore favored Internet readiness, I tend to agree with Gelernter, who laments the fact that students become too dependent on the computer and end up being weak writers who also lack basic math and language skills:

> With an Internet connection, you can gather the latest stuff from all over, but too many American high school students have never read one Mark Twain novel or Shakespeare play or Wordsworth poem, or a serious history of the U.S.; they are bad at science, useless at mathematics, hopeless at writ-

ing—but if they could only connect to the latest Web sites in Passaic and Peru, we'd see improvement.... And our skill-free children are overwhelmed by information even *without* the Internet. The glossy magazines and hundred-odd cable channels, the videotapes and computer CDs in most libraries and many homes—they need more information? (*Time,* May 25, 1998, p. 55)

Anyone who can "click" a mouse can surf the Internet—Web surfing is not the skill that our children need to succeed. If educators want to argue how important it is to be computer literate, I'd agree, but let's keep the issues straight. For America to stay on the cutting edge of technology, we need to develop and cultivate technological computer skills: repair, programming, debugging, and so on. Surfing the Net is something almost anyone can do and it requires very little special training.

As is evident from the plethora of useless Web sites, it does not take very much in the way of advanced knowledge to post and maintain a basic Web site, either. This being said, what then are the key aspects of computer technology that our children will need?

The Importance of Keyboarding/Typing Skills

First off, probably the most overlooked part of the whole computer revolution is keyboarding skills. Finger-typing and hunting and pecking for letters are not going to help your children at all when they are trying to take down notes in a class. Video game skills are not transferable. Even though there are programs that will translate the spoken word directly into print, they are expensive, not very accurate (especially for people who speak quickly), and impractical for taking notes during a class while the teacher is talking; the student can't speak his summary notes into a computer during the class while the professor is lecturing.

The only way to learn keyboarding is to take a keyboarding/ typing class. There are even computer programs that teach the skill. If your children's middle school does offer keyboarding, make sure your children sign up for it and learn how to type. If the school does not offer it, buy an inexpensive typing tutor program and encourage your children to learn how to type. I have to admit that I did not enjoy my typing class in high school, but it turned out to be one of the most useful skills that I picked up over the years.

Basic Proficiency

Second, even if your children's school does not require computer classes, be sure to have them sign up for a basic class in word processing, or a combination class that covers general applications such as database, spreadsheets, and Web site design in addition to word processing. If your child can master an all-in-one program like Microsoft Works (this includes a word-processing program, a drawing program, a spreadsheet and database program), he will have almost all the tools he needs for both high school and college. As for learning computer programming, unless your child is interested in learning computer languages, there will be very little use for this except the skills gained to learn any new language, whether that be a foreign language or a computer language. If your child is not technologically inclined, there is no need to learn anything beyond basic programming, if any at all.

Other Uses

Believe it or not, almost all the other things you could use computers for (research, surfing, E-mail) are not only easy to learn, but also best learned on an "as needed" basis.

High school students will often use the Internet to find information on writers and authors for an English assignment. No doubt if a student tried to find out everything he wanted to about Toni Morrison, he could, just by using the Internet to find all her books, her biography, reviews—even her E-mail address. But when these students go to college, they will need to learn a more specialized kind of research that requires knowledge of searching special databases that are usually available only through college libraries.

If the student needed to find obscure journal articles on Toni Morrison, a quick search of the MLA (Modern Language Association) Bibliography would turn up ten to twenty years' worth of academic journal articles. Once the student found this listing, he would have to cross-reference this list with the library's collection of journals (requiring another quick search through the library's computer catalog).

How would a student know how to do this? His first stop that freshman year in college would be to the college's reference librarian, who in ten minutes could show the student how to find the information. In fact, there is so much information available that only a highly trained reference librarian is really capable of finding it all in the first place. No student has the time to keep up with all the technological advances in academic research. So why spend time trying to keep abreast of this technology when there are already experienced specialists in the field of academic research who are at students' and professors' disposal in every university?

The Reality

In college, liberal arts students will mostly use the computer for E-mail, taking notes in class (if they can type quickly), writing papers, and for specialized science and math classes in which the professor will usually walk the students through what they need to know.

Some of the most able students I have known over the years still compose the old-fashioned way—in longhand—when writing papers. As odd as it sounds, by their very speed and ease of use, computers can weaken our writing skills. I call this phenomenon "automatic" (or autopilot) writing.

Automatic Writing

Let's look at a particular case. Your child is trying to write a five-to-six-page paper on Emily Dickinson and a few of her poems. So, like most students, he sits down the night before it is due, opens up a blank document on the computer, and stares at the cursor in the middle of the screen. After leafing through some of her poems, he begins to type whatever comes into his mind. Before he knows it, he has three single-spaced pages. Not bad, he says to himself. After a break, he glances over what he has written, reads another poem, and continues to pour out his thoughts. Once he realizes that he has five pages, he concludes that he has fulfilled the assignment and prints it out. If he is like most students, he will read it over quickly, make any obvious corrections, and then hand it in.

This is called "automatic" writing because what your child is actually doing is filling up space on a blank screen by writing whatever comes to mind with little regard for clarity, sentence structure, overall organization, and coherence. When he reads over his "draft," he finds it hard to correct because a typed paper looks so perfect that it is very difficult to get beneath the surface and look at the ideas behind the neatly printed words.

Now let's look at the archaic way of writing a paper. Before your child even starts writing, he reads through several poems and perhaps one book on Emily Dickinson's life to put her poems in a historical context. With a pack of index cards by his side, he takes notes and keeps a neat record of where these notes come from. He then makes an outline of what he is trying to prove. Let's say he decides to analyze how Dickinson portrays death in her poems. He then jots down a quick outline that includes a thesis statement, two topic sentences, and a list of which poems he will discuss under each subheading.

Finally, with all his notes spread out on the table in front of him along with some books, he opens up a pad of yellow legal paper and begins to let his hand produce thoughts. Odds are that he will put much more thought into what he is writing. Plus, he can cross out words, draw arrows from one part to another, not to mention examine his own work more critically because the paper looks like a work in progress rather than a finished product.

One of the benefits of writing by hand is that your child can lay out all the pages at once in front of him and view what his paper looks like. A computer, no matter how advanced, only lets you scroll down a paragraph or two at a time. It is nearly impossible to look at what he has on page three, and whether that ties in well with his analysis on page six and his thesis statement on page one. Whereas, if he has six sheets of legal paper in front of him, he could easily navigate through a long document, change sequences, and perform other editing tasks. Any high school teacher or college professor will tell you that students who type directly onto a computer do not write as well as those who handwrite at least part of their papers first and type them later.

Of course, word processors do come into play in the next stage. Once your child has most of his paper down, he types it into whatever program he has so he can spell-check, rearrange large sections, and refine as he goes. No computer can make your child a better writer—only a mechanically accurate one.

Do I Need to Buy a Computer for My Children?

Now that prices are so low for computers, they are becoming affordable to nearly everyone; even computers that come with lots of memory, a modem, a printer, a hard drive, and program bundles can be bought for under $1,000. With some creative research, you can probably buy a used computer from a college student for even less. Sure, it's convenient to use the Internet at home for research purposes or to find help with homework (in Appendix A, I have included some good Web sites for middle school and high school students as well as some powerful search engines that will aid research), but most high schools these days have computer stations set up in school.

Except for the convenience of being able to type a paper at home, I don't think you seriously handicap your children by not having a computer at home. Any student will tell you that he uses home computers more for computer games, Internet chat rooms, and E-mail than for academic purposes. On the other hand, I would still recommend having one at home because it can put you and your child in touch with teachers online, open up the many useful services on the Internet, and allow a child to carry documents (in disk format) from school to home and vice versa, to work on essays and projects.

As for laptop computers, sure, they are convenient, but note taking is a skill students still need to develop before they become too dependent on the computer. Also, most laptops are fairly fragile, so if your child is prone to dropping things, your expensive laptop will not hold up too well.

One of the strongest arguments for writing by hand is that for many major tests, computers are *not* allowed. For the SAT II writing test, for example, students must handwrite two essays in twenty minutes. The grader has to be able to read the essay or he will not be able to assign full credit, even if the work happens to be well written.

All Advanced Placement and International Baccalaureate tests have long writing sections on them. These tests are the most important tests that colleges will consider when students apply. Plus, students can earn college credit if they score well on these tests once they are admitted to college. If you can't write by hand, there is little hope of showing what you know.

In conclusion, computers are an integral part of our children's lives (and ours as well), but they are best used to supplement, not supplant, the basic skills all children need, such as crafting well-written sentences, having good penmanship, being proficient in math, and performing upper-level thought processes, none of which require computers in the first place! Computers are a tool for—but not the means to—academic success.

Chapter 9

Public versus Private School

Is One Inherently Better Than the Other?

Wouldn't it be nice if there were a straight answer to the question of which is better? Of course it's not that easy because you have to stop and think about what you mean by better. Better for getting into selective colleges? Better for learning core material? Better for talented actors who want a great acting program along with strong academics? Better for teaching basic skills and nurturing students so that they learn from square one how to succeed?

I have had the chance to reflect on this question both from my own personal experience and from my professional experience working in college admissions, where I visited hundreds of high schools around the country and read applications from thousands of high school students.

Although I was born in New York City and went to a small private school there until age six, all the rest of my elementary, middle school, and high school years were spent in public schools. I started out in elementary school in Chevy Chase, Maryland, which has one of the most incredible public high school systems in the country, and later attended third grade to high school in Westchester County, New York (Byram Hills High School), another fantastic school system. Some of my friends transferred to private schools in Westchester, and one or two transferred to prestigious boarding schools.

I can tell you from my perspective that in the honors and AP classes at my high school, we mastered the material and had teachers as inspiring as you could have at any school in the country. All the top students in my high school were accepted into the nation's most selective colleges right along with students from bigger-name secondary schools. Of course there were some weak teachers along the way, but they were the exception, not the rule. Although there were many weak students in the school, I didn't have many classes with them since they tended not to take the most advanced classes, so for the most part, I was in a school within a school, with the top students.

In addition, even though we were not a boarding school, I was good friends with my teachers then (they'd come to my athletic events, attend evening functions with students, invite students to their houses), and I still keep in touch with a handful of my high school teachers, some on a monthly basis. Two of them even helped me in my current role of department head. I can't think of any boarding school in which students developed closer relationships than I did with my teachers.

After I graduated from college and graduate school, I accepted a job as a teacher and coach at a small private boarding school in Putney, Vermont (the Putney School). I loved teaching in a place where the classes were very small (eight to twelve students per class), students were on a first-name basis with teachers, and you had the chance to get to know students as students, as athletes, and as people since I was also a dorm head for twenty-five girls. I was surrogate parent, coach, teacher, confidante, and counselor to many children. So I had the chance to observe firsthand the close relationships that develop at a boarding school.

After working at Putney, I spent four years in admissions. I learned the most about different schools from interviewing students who came from every different kind of school imaginable. There were those who loved their boarding school more than anything in the world, those who despised it, those who loved their neighborhood school, those who hated it, those who had attended both and had definite opinions on which was better, and so on.

Currently, I am a teacher and administrator at a private proprietorship day school in Florida. Since it is not a boarding school, I see students during the day, work with them after school, and then don't see them until the following morning.

So what is the answer? Simply put, whether a secondary school is private or public is not a determining factor as to whether it's better or worse. It's like comparing apples to oranges. There are many fine private schools and many terribly weak private schools, just as there are many fine public high schools and many abysmally poor ones. There are big private schools and small private schools. A common misconception is that private schools are always smaller and more intimate.

How Can You Find Out What a School Believes?

Now that it is clear that the distinction between good and bad secondary schools does not follow a private/public division, how can you evaluate the quality of a secondary school? The first step is to request the school catalog and read through it, paying attention to how the school sells itself. Most schools have a mission statement, which should give you a definite idea of what the school perceives as its selling point. Let's look at two different mission statements:

1. The _____ school accepts above average to gifted students and provides a rigorous environment with a classical focus that prepares students for admission to highly selective colleges.
2. The _____ school focuses on the whole development of the child. We provide a warm, nurturing environment, a

first-rate fine arts program, and a working farm where students learn a sense of responsibility and ownership.

Obviously number one is much more academic in nature, less nurturing, more rigorous, and makes no bones about basically accepting only top students and throwing lots of work their way to prepare them for the Ivies and like schools. Number two probably has some great teachers and strong classes, but concentrates more on the teacher-student relationship, arts program, and farm program. There is most likely less academic pressure.

Can you get into Harvard from either school? Of course! I will take up this point in the next section. The important consideration here is what kind of student your son or daughter is. Although you might prefer a high-achieving, self-motivated child whom you could send to school number one, if in fact you have a sensitive, artistic, kind, and diligent child, he or she would probably be miserably unhappy in school number one and would be better suited to number two.

Above all, you want to select a high school that fits your child's capabilities and personality. A highly competitive high school might actually stifle a bright but sensitive student, whereas a school more suited to his needs might bring out his academic talents. What you want to ask yourself is, What are my child's interests and talents, what kind of temperament does he have (self-directed, lazy, independent?), and what kind of school would be likely to develop his talents? If your son is a computer genius, don't send him to a tiny private school that has no technology program whatsoever.

One terrific resource for researching private schools and making the right match for you and your child is a new Web site: www.edu-metrics.com. For a reasonable fee, this site provides critical data for more than 1,400 private secondary schools along with an on-line advisory service for individual inquiries. A subscription also gives you access to a private secondary schools newsletter with articles about trends in private school education and issues to consider when selecting a private school.

If your child has many different interests, sometimes nothing will beat the local public school for sheer number of options. At a large public high school, you find programs from the vocational level to Westinghouse research. Oftentimes public high schools are so well funded that they have tremendous theater or sports facilities. By contrast, many fine private schools have much smaller libraries, facilities, and options.

The second investigative step is to request the secondary school's college profile, which it sends to every college along with student applications. Most parents do not realize that almost every school in the country has this college profile. Remember, you will need to contact the guidance or college department of the high school rather than the admissions department, since this document is not used as a public relations tool, but rather as an informative document for colleges.

What does the profile include? It usually starts with a description of the school and neighborhood, the income level and racial composition of the area, the facilities on campus, and an overview of the academic program. It then provides a wealth of concrete information: what universities students from previous classes have been accepted to, average SAT I and SAT II scores, the latter by subject, average AP scores, the number of National Merit Semi-Finalists and Finalists, any other national awards that students win, plus all the different academic course work available to students.

By comparing these college profiles, you will quickly be able to compare a particular school's admissions brochure (which often is a slick publicity-oriented piece designed for attracting and enrolling students) with its college brochure to see if they really follow through on their promise. For example, if you read the first mission statement above and then saw on the profile that the majority of students attend state schools and only a small percentage attend selective schools, you'd quickly realize that they were mostly bluff with little follow-through. You might be surprised to find out that from school number two, half the class attends highly competitive schools.

In admissions material, the school's job is to sell itself to the public. In its college profile, the school is trying to present an honest portrait to colleges. Even if the school makes its profile glossy or attractive, it still cannot make up the hard information that must be included. They cannot make up high SAT I and SAT II averages, nor AP scores, nor where students attend college. This is why it is imperative to compare these two publications when you are judging a school.

Finally, once you have compared several schools through their published materials, you need to visit campuses on an official visit with your child. Have an interview, ask questions, talk to students (who are usually unfailingly honest and direct), get an impression of the campus, observe classes to see if they are challenging or not. You will find out more during a brief visit, even in terms of the atmosphere of the place, than you would if you studied the official publications for years. On paper a school might sound great, yet if you tour the school, it may be immediately obvious that your child would never fit in.

How Much Can a School Really Change Your Child?

I think sometimes parents have unrealistic expectations about the role schools should have in their child's life. While there is no doubt that especially at boarding schools, the school certainly plays a big role in forming a child's personality and intellect, I disagree with the concept that a school's primary responsibility is to serve as a surrogate parent.

I know too many parents who throw up their hands in despair when their children reach puberty and decide that they simply cannot handle them. Over the years, I have seen parents who worked too many hours to spend quality time with their children; others had family problems that prevented them from giving the love and attention all children need. Even where

I work now, I speak to parents every day who complain to me that if their children don't improve in terms of behavior and academic achievement they are going to pull them out of our school and enroll them in a military academy.

I may be old-fashioned, but I believe that parents are largely responsible for the emotional development and behavior of their children. Let me give you some concrete examples about parent attitudes from the various schools where I have worked.

Once, in response to a summer reading assignment on *Little Women*, I received a complaint call from a parent who vehemently insisted that her seventh-grade son could not read *Little Women* because he was a boy and did not want to read a book about girls. Besides, she added, how could I expect her son to read such an embarrassing book in public—what would his friends think of him? At first I didn't think she could be serious, particularly about the danger of reading the book in public lest his friends think he was a sissy, or, worse yet in her eyes, gay. Unfortunately, she was not kidding.

I reasoned with her. I told her that, first of all, there were plenty of male characters in the book despite the title (she had never read the book) and besides, since her son sees girls every day, why shouldn't he want to read about how they think and act? Then I mentioned that plenty of girls spend their entire adolescence reading Hardy Boys books, just as many boys enjoy Nancy Drew mysteries.

Is *Huckleberry Finn* only for boys? No matter what logical argument I presented, this mother just could not get over the fact that her son would somehow be traumatized by being forced to read this book. She even asked if he could read *Little Men* instead, to which I replied in the negative since the first two weeks of school would be spent going over *Little Women*, not *Little Men*.

Finally I realized that I could not convince her, but during the conversation, it became clear to me that her son really hated reading to begin with and was having difficulty with the book. Rather than argue with her, I turned the conversation toward helping her think of ways to read aloud with him so that he could understand the book. When I finally hung up, it dawned on me: This mother was subverting her own child's education. I don't think her son much cared about reading *Little Women,* but even if he did, it is *her* job, not a teacher's, to support the school and reinforce the importance of reading. Even if her son thought it was a sissy book to read, she should be the one to convince him that it is important in life to read and understand about the opposite sex, and that there is always something to learn from any book, in this case about the American Civil War, not just the characters. After all, the book is about the effects of the war on families, not about some random girls hanging out at the mall.

Think how difficult it would be for a teacher to educate this woman's son and teach him about gender roles and attitudes toward female classmates when he comes from a home where his own mother is unable to impart these basic values—in fact, she might not even believe in them herself. Granted, a school can go a long way toward educating and enlightening a child's mind, but how can it educate the parents? So long as the child lives at home, everything the school teaches can be undermined by the parents if they are determined enough to subvert the school's efforts.

Let me recount one more example regarding summer reading assignments. This one involved a parent whose child was entering ninth grade. I assigned to this class of ninth-graders the difficult job of reading Homer's *Iliad* and then producing short newspaper accounts of each of the twenty-four books complete with newspaper headlines, bylines, and lead articles or editorials, such as "Prettiest Woman in All of Ilium Carried Off by the Dashing Paris: Greeks Say They Want Her Back." I anticipated complaints about the difficulty level of the reading, but what I was not expecting was the indignant attack I encountered when I heard from yet another mother.

She called me about three weeks before the beginning of school to inform me that there was no way I could expect her daughter to do the reading since she spent the whole summer in camp. When I asked her how many weeks the camp lasted, she said that it was eight, but then the whole family went on a two-week vacation. Could her daughter not read at camp? I asked her. For me, camp was one of my favorite times of the year to read because there was no schoolwork to interfere with my outside reading.

"Read in camp!" she cried. "She's *busy,* and besides, they go on camping trips." What about vacation? No, that wouldn't work either because they go to Europe and see many different places and family members. Again I thought about how I had read scores of books while I was in Europe, both in the places I stayed and in trains, on buses, in beautiful outdoor plazas, and in parks; reading in foreign places during sight-seeing breaks, it seems to me, is one of the greatest joys in life.

Finally, I realized that all I could do was tell her that her daughter had to read the book, no matter how it got done, and that I was not going to figure it out for her. Since we were going to spend the first few weeks on the *Iliad* and the summer assignment would be a sizable part of the first-quarter grade, I told her that the logistics were up to her, but that she needed to get a copy of the book to her daughter so she could complete the project.

Where are this parent's priorities? If you believe in education, school cannot interfere with summer vacation; it can only enhance it. How can knowledge and intellectual inquiry interfere with summer camp? Any child can meet all the requirements of his camp and still have some time either during rest hour or at night before lights-out to do required summer reading. Learning can and should take place both at school and during breaks from school. Think how that mother's attitude stifles her child's understanding of why learning is important. I know in a case like this that my parents, because they believed in education above all else, would have done everything in their power to back the school. If I had argued that I couldn't read in camp, their response would have been, "You can either read in camp or stay home for the summer and complete the summer reading." Almost any child, when faced with this response, would figure out a way to get the reading done at camp.

The point is that not all parents, even those who spend thousands of dollars to send their kids to the finest schools, believe in learning for the sake of learning. If this student's parents were at all literary or intellectual, they not only would have encouraged their daughter to read, they would have brought along books for themselves on their European trip so their children would have seen that reading is important. I think back to my childhood and I can recall my whole family sitting around the living room or bedroom with the cat, everyone reading a book silently until either a question or an interesting part came up, in which case we'd read it aloud and discuss it. If I had a summer reading project, my parents would be the first ones to take me to a library and help me find materials—in short, they would *enable* me to do the assignment. This parent was doing the opposite; rather than enabling her child, she was trying to make excuses on behalf of her child as to why she shouldn't do the reading.

The reason I bring up these anecdotes is to illustrate my point that a school can do only so much. Sure, military schools can improve a child's discipline and self-esteem. Yes, boarding schools have dedicated faculty who spend so much time with students in the classroom, on the athletic field, and in the dorms that they do have a tremendous influence on many students. However, they are not parents, they are teachers. The roles of parent and teacher should not be identical.

I think you as parents can expect a school to challenge your children's intellects, set a good example of behavior, and improve study skills and interpersonal habits, but it cannot take a psychologically disturbed teen and turn him into the perfect child.

As parents, we need to foster a love of learning at home and do everything we can to support a school, not try constantly to undermine a school's efforts. Teach your children through example: Read with them, to them, discuss politics with them, engage their minds in debate, help them through emotionally hard times, but don't relinquish to a school your role as parent.

Let me give one more example, this time on the behavioral front. When I caught two students who not only disrupted class for the entire period while a substitute was present, but also at the end of the class lied by giving false names to the teacher, I spoke to them in my office. Then I assigned them both to detention and called their parents to explain what they had done. Both girls were on the soccer team and the detention meant that they would have to miss a game.

The first parent was horrified at what her daughter had done. She thanked us for making her miss the soccer game and said that it would teach her daughter a valuable lesson about accountability. The second parent directed all her anger toward the school. How was her daughter supposed to miss a big soccer game? It was only a substitute, so what did it matter? She went so far as to accuse the school of being unfair. She was paying for this school so her child could participate in sports, so how could we take this right away from her?

By now you get the idea. Parent number one had the appropriate attitude, while parent number two was out of line. By all means hold a school to high standards of excellence, but do not expect the school to fill your role as parent.

What About Cost?

Though at first glance it might appear that private school is always more expensive, consider two major factors: (1) Many parents pay sky-high taxes to live in a district like Scarsdale, New York, where the public schools are first-rate, so in effect they are paying for public school; and (2) though tuition at a boarding school might seem prohibitive at times, remember that all strong private schools give both financial aid for needy students and sometimes honors merit scholarships as well. There-fore, if you compare any two students from an elite boarding school like Exeter or Hotchkiss, what you'd find would be similar to what you find if you asked the people on either side of your airplane seat what they paid for the flight—one student might have a free ride while the other could be paying full tuition, room, and board.

The main factor to keep in mind is that if your child is intellectually gifted, do not rule out any school based on cost alone. In fact, the less money you make and the lower your socioeconomic status, the more likely it is that elite boarding schools will be interested in your child.

Think of matters from the school's perspective: A school like Hotchkiss gets all sorts of applications from well-to-do and established families, and many of those privileged applicants are gifted students. Hotchkiss will always have a good selection of these students to choose from. What it doesn't have are a lot of gifted student applicants from low-income or minority backgrounds because, more often than not, these students self-select themselves out of the process by thinking that they are not good enough to be accepted and that the school is financially out of their reach. Remember: Neither of these assumptions is true! If you have a gifted child and you have limited resources, think of yourself as having a valuable commodity on your hands.

No private high school, no matter how elite, wants to be filled with an overwhelmingly high percentage of white, upper-crust students when they are spending tens of thousands of dollars a year to recruit gifted minority and low-income students from around the country. The key word is diversity: All private schools have to market the fact that they have a "diverse" student body, which means economic diversity, geographic diversity, racial diversity, and so on. The only way they can attract these kinds of students is to give out copious amounts of financial aid and scholarship dollars.

Another fact to file away is that in general, the more elite or prestigious the private school, the bigger the endowment and the more money it is able to award to needy students. Compare the endowment of schools like Andover and Exeter to small, little-known private schools and you will be shocked to discover how much money a year they award in financial aid. Of course, there are also small private schools that have been lucky enough to build up their endowments through generous alumni giving, or sometimes due to one huge gift (i.e., the Peddie School in New Jersey) and therefore can award generous financial aid.

The school where I currently work is privately owned. Though we do not have a large endowment, the proprietor himself funds about twenty intellectually gifted students a year from our local area. These scholarship students greatly enrich the campus by bringing their enthusiasm for learning as well as their academic and extracurricular talents to the campus. As long as they maintain a high enough GPA, they receive full tuition for their four years of high school.

The moral is that although it makes sense to investigate and compare schools' costs, you also must remember to take into account that many fine schools offer generous aid packages, so you should never eliminate a school based on cost alone. You also want to avoid a situation where you are paying the cost of school twice over. For example, if you are living in an area like Scarsdale in Westchester County, New York, unless you have unlimited funds you need to think twice about paying $25,000 a year extra to send your child to an expensive boarding school. Many parents in a case like this who do opt for the private school decide to live in a slightly less expensive county so they don't have to subsidize the local school through taxes and then pay again to send their children to school.

Is It Easier to Get into College from Private or Public School?

Unfortunately, a great majority of parents who send their children to private school assume that along with their tuition dollars comes an assurance that their children will be accepted to any college in the country.

Let me state the point plainly: The mere fact of attending a private school versus a public school does not translate into a better chance of getting into a highly selective college. In fact, from many elite private schools where the competition to be in the top 10 percent of the senior class is very tough, it may actually hurt one's chances of being accepted into a very selective school.

Let's examine briefly why this is so. The highly selective colleges like Harvard, Yale, and Dartmouth have the luxury of receiving an incredibly high number of applications for an incredibly low number of spaces in the class. Typically, at Dartmouth College, where I worked, we received between 12,000 and 15,000 applications a year, of which we accepted roughly 2,500 and enrolled roughly 1,250. Since all these colleges are compared by publications like *U.S. News & World Report* and dozens of other companies and guidebooks that rank colleges, they are very concerned with statistics. One of the most important statistics to show selectivity besides average SAT scores is the number of students they accept who are in the top 10 percent of their graduating class.

If you examine the Ivies and comparable schools, you will notice that they all accept between 85 percent and 97 percent of their students from the top 10 percent of their high school graduating class. But now let's think about it—imagine you are a student at a school like Andover or St. Paul's, where there are many bright, motivated, and high-scoring students all vying for the top space in their class. Then compare this situation to one at a big urban public school where there might be 1,000 students in the senior class, but only a handful of bright over-achievers in all honors and AP classes who are competing for the top spaces.

In fact, the competition is even more pointed, because another statistic that colleges like to brag about is the percentage of valedictorians and salutatorians they accept—again, to cite Dartmouth's typical numbers, anywhere from 35 to 45 percent of the incoming freshman class graduated either number one or number two in their high school class. Thus, assuming that these colleges are looking at two students with equally impressive standardized test scores but one is number one in a big urban high school and the other is just out of the top 10 percent of the class at Andover, it is my experience that they will select the public-school student every time.

First of all, choosing the public-school valedictorian bolsters the school's statistics since it looks on the surface as though it is being more selective because the number of high school valedictorians stays high, and, second, the odds are that the public-school student will be from a lower economic background (or at least less privileged) so the search criteria for "diversity" will be met as well.

Now it would seem that it is always better to go to a public school, but the other factor to keep in mind is that if the school is not very good, the odds are that your children will not have the correspondingly high standardized test scores that they need to get into top colleges, whatever their rank may be.

From my statistical analysis, it turned out that the acceptance rate from all public schools taken together and from all private schools is almost identical. That is to say, all the factors I mentioned above tend to cancel each other out, so that students from both public and private schools have an equal chance at getting accepted to the college of their choice.

In short, do not opt to send your children to private school just because you think it will increase their odds of getting accepted to college. Naturally, there are other good reasons to decide to send your children to private school: You can pick a school that is very well matched to your child's talents and academic needs; you can pick a school that has a very small class size; the intellectual environment and the overall quality of the student body may be much higher than those at a public school—all of these are valid reasons to select a private school.

Keep in mind that private schools manipulate their own statistics so they can "prove" to the public that their students do indeed have a better chance of getting accepted at top colleges. Many New York City private schools, for example, will say that over 50 percent of their seniors are accepted into Ivy League schools. Well, that may be, but they do not have a higher acceptance rate to each of those schools. In other words, if the average acceptance rate for a certain college is 20 percent, usually just about 20 percent of its students are accepted into that college. What makes the 50 percent figure so high is the fact that almost all of their students apply to selective colleges, so of course a greater percentage of them end up going. Add to this the fact that these private schools preselect those who they feel, based on IQ and other tests, will be good applicants to selective schools. These schools are actually selective themselves, so they may accept only 25 percent of those who apply to get in, and then funnel these students on to selective colleges.

Therefore, the fact that a high number of students eventually are accepted to Ivy League schools does not mean that they were accepted at a higher rate. If you want to do the math yourself, request the statistics from schools you are looking at from the college guidance office. Ask them how many applied to Harvard versus how many were accepted. At least then you are comparing apples to apples at each school you look at.

From all the applicants I have seen over the years, it is encouraging to note that some of the most intellectually gifted ones came from obscure public schools in far-away states, not from name-brand private schools or strong public schools. Real intellectual power and love of learning know no bounds, and these attributes cross ethnic, economic, social, and political lines.

As parents, your job is to think of your child as a person,

both as a student in the classroom and as someone who participates in certain extracurricular activities. Then, when choosing a secondary school, whether public or private, you need to do the research, request the information I mention earlier in the chapter, talk to parents and other students, and try to make an informed decision about what kind of school would best fit your child's needs. As far as getting into college is concerned, you need not put this factor in the forefront because, as unlikely as it may seem, it is really the least important of all factors.

Chapter 10

Tutoring: Is It Really Worth It?

Specific Subject Tutoring

Though I don't put much stock in tutoring for standardized tests, I do think oftentimes tutoring in individual subjects can be a good idea, depending upon the surrounding circumstances. Before investing in a subject tutor, I would recommend encouraging your child to go on-line. In Appendix A, I list many helpful homework Web sites that could be utilized before a tutor is considered.

Let's say your child does well in all his subjects except one. That's a good sign that he does not have a serious learning disability that interferes with his learning across the board. Before getting a tutor, ask yourself some pertinent questions: Is this the first time my child has ever had trouble in this subject, or is this a long-standing problem? Is this a particularly difficult class (say, calculus) where many students are struggling? Is my child one of the only ones having trouble, or is the problem widespread?

I mention these points because many parents have a knee-jerk reaction of getting a tutor before they investigate for themselves what the problem is. The first recourse should always be speaking to the teacher to find out what he recommends. The teacher might tell you that your child in fact has great ability, but is only doing two minutes of homework a night rather than the forty-five-minute minimum that is required to do A-level work. Or he might tell you that your child is doing fine now but just had one or two aberrant test scores that lowered his grade. Or he might tell you that there may be a learning difficulty (perhaps reading, or processing) that is interfering with learning and he can recommend testing for specific problems.

No matter what you ultimately decide to do, remember that the teacher is your closest link to the day-to-day work habits of your child and is also a specialist in that particular subject. Too often I see parents bypassing teachers and running out to get a tutor at the first sign of a weak grade. Why bypass your most valuable resource—your child's teacher?

As for finding specific tutors, the best bargain is always high-achieving students in the high school who are looking for ways to earn extra money. Sure, you can pay an adult or a teacher to tutor your child, but there are several good arguments for going with a peer tutor rather than an adult tutor.

The first is that, especially for middle school students, one of the best ways to motivate children for success is to see a successful high school role model who can relay the concept that studying is cool. Oftentimes young students will forge very positive friendships with high school students, so the help they deliver is on two levels: academic and personal.

The second is that these high school students have already had many of the same teachers, exams, and classes that your middle-schooler is working with now, so they really are the experts in terms of tutoring for specific information. If you had already passed through Mr. Muller's eighth-grade algebra class, it would be much easier for you as a tenth-grader to go back and assist a young student taking the same class.

Finally, the high school students are a bargain. While you might pay them only ten to twenty dollars an hour depending on ability (some very coveted ones deserve the fifty dollars an hour they charge), compare that to a teacher or a tutor, who can charge anywhere from $20 to $450 an hour! You certainly don't want to throw money away.

How can you tell if you are relying too much on tutors? As a rule, if your child is having trouble in two or more subjects and is not improving, there might be a problem more serious than lack of studying. The general rule is that you want to use tutors to help your child through trouble spots in certain classes, but you never want to rely on tutors to the point that your child can do his homework only with a tutor. Think of tutoring as a way to make your child more independent (assuming there is no learning disability, a topic we will take up in Chapter 12); tutoring has its place, yet it should never render the child unable to do the work himself.

SAT Tutoring

It is useful to weigh the benefits of a seasoned, older tutor with those of a younger, less experienced tutor. In some cases, it will definitely be worthwhile to go with a more experienced tutor because he will be able both to serve a nurturing role (i.e., allaying a fear of math) and also to pinpoint common problems in a certain area that your child may be experiencing.

Just to aid those of you who are new to the standardized testing world, the SAT I is what most of you have always known as the SAT, the Scholastic Aptitude Test, which has undergone many changes in recent years. Though the story is complicated, all you need to know is that the College Board has replaced the "aptitude" part of the title with "assessment," so SAT is now an acronym for Scholastic Assessment Test. In addition, they have "recentered" the test (scored 200–800) so that the true average is now a 500 and the test results fall into a bell curve of evenly distributed scores from 500 down to 200 and from 500 up to 800. To those who are used to the "old" scores, the new scores tend to sound inflated. What used to be a 720 verbal score on the old scale is now an 800 on the new scale, to give you one example. Following is a conversion scale from old scores to new scores.

Original Verbal	Recentered Verbal	Original Math	Recentered Math
800	800	800	800
790	800	790	800
780	800	780	800
770	800	770	790
730	800	730	730
720	790	720	720
670	730	670	660
660	720	660	650
650	710	650	650
600	670	600	600
590	660	590	600
580	650	580	590
400	480	400	440
300	380	300	340
200	230	200	200

The SAT II tests used to be called "achievement" tests. Except for the fact that their scores are recentered as well, the tests are largely the same as before—one-hour tests in a specific subject matter (more than twenty are available) as opposed to the three-hour SAT I.*

The question we need to look at is, is it necessary to hire a tutor for your son or daughter? There has been a barrage of media attention focusing on this very question. The *New York Times Magazine* ran an influential cover story on the SAT I that followed several students who had been tutored at $450 an hour for the SATs. Other New York parents see these children getting tutored by outrageously expensive tutors and fold to the peer pressure to do the same for their own children so they will not be at any disadvantage. Although the article did not openly condemn parents who paid outrageous amounts of

---

*Although it was the case that many colleges used to require only the SAT I, nowadays almost all selective colleges require both the SAT I and three SAT II tests.

money for tutoring, it did explain why students felt that they had no choice: If all their friends did it, they would be behind if they didn't.

Since the SAT is designed to be an aptitude test, it would seem that tutoring really cannot help, but, alas, if you are at all familiar with the test, there is no doubt that being acquainted with the test's format and brushing up on the specific areas of English and math it covers can dramatically improve test scores.

In fact, I would argue that tutoring is much more effective in the math section of the SAT, since a finite amount of material is tested. If you practice the same types of problems over and over, you are bound to increase your scores. The verbal section, however, is designed to test reading skills. I know of very few people who were not strong readers from childhood who scored exceptionally well on the verbal section of the SAT, no matter how much they were tutored.

The good news is that you do not need a tutor or an SAT class to prepare you for these tests if you do not want to hire one or can't afford one. The key is *familiarity* with the test, and that can be obtained by buying College Board publications like *10 Real SAT Tests* and practicing them section by section. Once you know all the directions and all the question types, your score goes up around fifty points just because you don't lose any time reading the directions and you can spend that extra time answering questions correctly. In addition, once you are familiar with the test, you can also buy for a modest price prep books by companies like Barron's or the Princeton Review, both of which are helpful publications filled with tips and strategies for taking the SAT.

This is the strategy I recommend for the majority of students who throw away thousands of dollars a year on tutoring and name-brand SAT classes when almost all of the test-taking techniques are available on the Internet (check out the College Board's official site, www.ets.org) and in widely available publications.

Why, then, would anyone enroll in an expensive SAT class?

One reason, I guess, is that if you have the money, it doesn't seem like such a big expense. Another may be that, if you are just plain too lazy to do the work yourself, a class or tutor forces you to spend the time to familiarize yourself with the test even if you really don't want to. (I suspect that the majority of students who enroll in these classes fall into this category.) Also, students erroneously assume that since their friends are doing it, they will do worse on the test and put themselves at an unfair disadvantage if they do not enroll as well.

As parents, you have the power to lobby your child's school to provide subsidized SAT tutoring for those who are interested. The money tends to be money well spent, since the school usually gets students with higher scores and the parents are happy that the cost is, at least in part, subsidized. Many New York City schools, alarmed by the number of students who were paying big bucks for private tutors and SAT classes, decided that their lower-income students were at a disadvantage; these schools are starting to contract directly with Stanley Kaplan and Princeton Review to offer SAT prep classes right on their campuses.

If you are going to spend the money for a class, at least the amount of money is modest compared to the amount for private tutoring. Rather than pay someone $450 an hour, I'd recommend paying $20 an hour to a motivated classmate of your child's, particularly an older one who has already scored well on the SAT. Then at least you will keep your cost down and make a compromise between having your child do all the work on his own and paying a lot of money for private classes or tutoring.

As for SAT II tests, you have every right as a parent to ask your child's teachers what they are doing to prepare him. The majority of highly selective colleges request a student's three strongest SAT II scores. Most strong high schools already give out practice SAT II tests in specific classes so students can practice the material. In case your school is not as up to date as it should be, you need to advocate the importance of SAT II tests.

I argue that SAT II tests are at least as important as, if not more so than, SAT I tests because they help to standardize grades in a particular subject from any school in the country.

If student number one gets an A in biology and a 750 on the SAT II test while student number two gets an A but scores a 480, any college would immediately realize that student number one came from a much more rigorous class and learned much more biology than did student number two. Admissions officers would also note that student number two's grade was very inflated since a 480 does not reflect a very strong knowledge of the subject matter.

Most highly competitive high schools report average SAT II scores by subject, so it is clearly in their best interest to require teachers to prepare students for these one-hour tests. And since the test is only one hour long and has a clearly defined set of material that is tested, the SAT IIs are much easier to study for on your own than the SAT I. Since students generally take only one or two tests a year (especially if they start early on in ninth grade taking one or two), the amount of preparation is not overwhelming. There are any number of study guides available for these tests. Before you get a tutor, I would suggest that you investigate the results from your children's teachers and ask them how they prepare the children. You can look at the averages from years past to get an idea of how students at your school are scoring.

If the scores seem low or you know a teacher is weak, hire a fellow student for a modest price to tutor your child, or buy him the appropriate books (found in the SAT I and SAT II study guides section of almost any major bookstore, or order directly from the College Board in Princeton, New Jersey) so in the spring, a few weeks before the test, he can find out what he needs to master before the test date.

Chapter 11

Tracking: Am I Doing My Child a Favor or Hurting His Chances for College Admission?

What Is Tracking and How Early Does It Start?

Tracking refers to separate levels of classes for students at different levels. Therefore, students can be on an "advanced" track, a "regular" track, or a "slow" track, in the most general sense. The problem is that many schools try to judge a student's ability too early in his schooling and mistakenly hold back deserving students or advance slower students. Tracking can start as early as preschool, when some students are held back a full year, or as late as middle school or high school. It is supposed to be based on the student's intelligence, but, as we will see, this evaluation of students is no easy task.

There is no universal standard for judging intelligence, for even the most advanced IQ tests do not tell the whole story. The more we discover about learning styles and learning differences, the more we realize how complicated it is to evaluate intelligence. One thing IQ tests definitely do *not* measure is intellectual curiosity. It is therefore perfectly possible to have a very bright student who has absolutely no desire to learn what is being taught in school, just as it is possible to have a student of limited intelligence who simply loves learning.

The fact that many elementary schools try to separate students into different tracks in the first place shows that you as a parent need to be aware of your own child's ability relative to his placement starting from when he begins school.

What Are These Programs Called?

It's hard even to compare the process in different schools around the country because terminology differs from one school to another, and these tracking programs go by many different names.

The first task, then, is at least to become familiar with some of the nomenclature. In the most general sense, tracking programs are referred to as "pull-out" programs because you have to pull a child out of one level to put him into another level. Schools use terms like *enrichment program, gifted and talented, gifted, honors, accelerated,* and *advanced* to identify the higher level of study, while words like *regular, grade-level,* and *standard* apply to the middle level of course work. *Trade* and *vocational* refer to course work that leads to a basic high school degree with a practical bent toward working full time.

At the high school level, the two crowning programs are Advanced Placement (AP) classes and the International Baccalaureate (IB) program, which represent the highest level of study before college. Though the programs are extremely different from each other (and some would say that AP is a discrete set of classes, not a program), they are still both considered the most advanced course work you can take before college. To make matters more confusing, some big high schools offer both programs, so students need to navigate among all the possible choices.

With all these programs out there, it is vitally important that you not lose sight of a basic goal: to follow closely your child's tracking so that he will be placed in classes *appropriate to his ability level.* This placement varies by subject, so it is fine for a student to be in advanced math but regular English if math is indeed his strength. You want to be very sensitive about pushing a child too early in school because pushing may have the opposite effect from the one you might intend.

For example, let's say your daughter is a fun-loving, friendly sixth-grader who loves sports, socializing, and math, but hates reading and has trouble sitting in one place long enough to complete a book. Let's suppose that by her standardized test scores you can tell that she is much stronger in math and analytical areas than she is in verbal and reading areas. Although she might be able to handle honors or gifted-level classes in English, if you force her too early into reading-intensive classes, you might end up stifling any positive feelings she may have had toward reading. It would be a much better strategy at this early age to let her accelerate in math and science but keep her at the regular level for reading.

How Is a Student's Academic Level Determined?

As a parent, you always want to communicate with your children's schools to see what criteria they use for placement. Some schools use only standardized test scores, some use grades, some use teacher recommendations, some use IQ tests, some use writing samples or placement tests, some use a combination of items—the process varies so much from school to school that there is no way to generalize here except to say that the school should be able to define for you how it makes the decision.

Once you find out the school's procedure, you have to draw a fine line between advocating for your child and supporting the school's decisions regarding placement. From the school's perspective, they see their share of pushy parents. These parents always insist that their children are geniuses and a blessing to the school.

Of course, not every parent is going to be correct when he tries to judge his child's abilities objectively, so there does need to be some measure of outside objectivity. As a parent, you want to avoid being so aggressive with the school that you become a dreaded presence.

Let's start at the middle school level. If there are honors-level classes and regular-level classes, first see how the school places your child and what criteria they used to make that placement. Compare your view of your child with the school's; if they are relying heavily on standardized testing, take a good look yourself to see if there might not be some truth in the school's assessment. One test that is used quite often in placement at private schools is the SSAT, simply because the majority of private schools require the test for admission, so it is therefore very easy to use the verbal and math scores for placement.

If, on the SSAT your child scores in the tenth percentile for reading and verbal and in the eightieth percentile for math, it is reasonable for the school to assign a regular-level English class with an advanced-level math class. By the same token, if your child scores in the ninetieth percentile for reading and only in the fifteenth percentile for math, then it seems reasonable to assign advanced English and regular math.

But what happens if you think the test is somehow wrong? Let's take the low reading score in the first example above. What if your child has been a devoted reader for years and you think the score does not reflect his ability? If he's reading *Great Expectations* in the seventh grade, you should have a fairly good indication that the actual reading is not the problem.

What if he was sick when he took the test, or what if he didn't understand the test format and left too many questions blank, or omitted a whole section by mistake, or filled in the circles incorrectly? There could be a whole gamut of problems that might have interfered with an accurate test score.

In a case like this, there are several recourses. If you think there was some kind of problem with the mechanics of taking the test, first have your child take the test again. At least this will clear up the mystery of whether a technical problem interfered. Second, ask to meet with the English teacher and have your child discuss the books he has read in the past year or so. Oftentimes a teacher will be so impressed with a student's obvious reading ability and affinity for language that she will decide to override the school's decision and accept the child into her class. Third, ask if there is a placement test given by the school that your child could take. Finally, if your child has a long tradition of A's with great report cards in English, present a case to the school as to why you think he should be in honors-level English.

If nothing you say convinces the school, another step you can try is to work out a compromise with the teacher where your child is accepted only conditionally. The "condition" could be that he be allowed to start the year in that class, but at any point if the teacher feels he is not working up to level or he is significantly below the performance of other students in the class, he has to transfer out. This procedure at least gives the child a chance to prove himself.

This probation gives both the school and the family a compromise that will work out one way or the other. If the student truly should be in the class, he will do well and excel, therefore the teacher would be glad to have him. If the testing was accurate and he in fact had a reading problem and proves to be behind the rest of the class, he can say he tried and transfer into the next class. Very likely, the child will be relieved to end the pressure of being in a class of stronger readers.

What if Your Child Is on the Border?

What if your child is on the border between honors and regular classes? In this case, you really need to compare your child's motivation and interest levels by subject to distinguish the areas where it would be better to accelerate and the areas where it would be better to stay at the regular level. There are several other factors that need to be considered as well:

1. How mature is your child?
2. How diligent is your child? How likely is he to buckle down and complete homework?
3. How interested is your child in a particular subject?
4. What, if any, are his eventual career goals?
5. How good is the teacher?
6. How does your child compare to his classmates?
7. How much additional homework is there in the advanced sections and what does the school recommend for the heaviest class load?

Remember, at the sixth-to-eighth-grade level you don't want to force your child into a pattern of so much homework a night because of the high number of honors classes he's taking that he learns to hate school. As we have said, the middle school years are vitally important in encouraging a lifelong love of hands-on, experiential learning, not just rote reading, writing, and math. Look at the big picture: If your child has a natural gift in foreign languages, let him take the more advanced level in middle school so that he can even start a second language like Latin or Greek by the time he gets to high school. If she is a math whiz, it may be worth it to push ahead in math, since that means she may have a chance to advance as far as AB or BC calculus in high school and get college credit.

It is a very good idea to look ahead to your school's high school curriculum and then figure backward to see which areas it seems worthwhile to accelerate in. If the school is known for its tremendous science and technology program, maybe it will be worthwhile to push ahead in science.

The most important factor to keep in mind during all these deliberations is that if your child is truly not interested or gifted in a certain subject, don't push him to advance. Rather than looking across the board at whether your child should be in all honors, or all regular, classes, treat the decision in a subject-by-subject fashion. It is a much smarter strategy to push your child in the three areas where he is the most gifted and let him stay at the regular level in other classes until other interests develop.

On the other hand, it is also important to push your child to try different activities, both in and out of school, precisely because middle school-age students don't necessarily themselves know what they like and dislike or where their true talents lie. It is always a good idea to leave all the doors to exploration open while at the same time recognizing real strengths and weaknesses.

One of the biggest mistakes parents make is forcing the school to accept their children into classes that are really over their head. Don't make your children suffer because of some pre-conceived notion of success you may have.

During recent parent meetings over academic probation, I had one parent insist that his daughter take geometry as a ninth-grader because he had just read an article on the importance of a math and computer background in the current job market. The problem was that his daughter had a relatively low math ability and was not at all interested—she was a very able English and foreign language student, but had no interest in math.

It would have been a major mistake to force her to advance in math, particularly at the behest of the father, who saw his own image of what his daughter *should* be like, not how she really was. Luckily, in this case sound advice prevailed and we convinced him that his daughter would be much happier taking honors-level classes in all areas but math. This choice would in no way preclude a future interest in math, but at least it didn't overburden the student with too much math at too early an age.

What Can You Do if Immaturity Is Holding Your Child Back Academically?

The most common problem with students at the middle school level is that a bright student who is rightly placed in all honors-level classes ends up with straight C's. Why? It is probably because he is so immature that he does not listen in class, distracts others, and does not follow through diligently with homework assignments. After a year of lackluster performance, it is within the school's right to place that child in regular classes because: (1) He is not succeeding; and (2) he is distracting other students from achieving at the highest possible level.

What can you do? In this case, you really have to side with the school and acknowledge your child's lack of maturity. There could be a variety of problems: emotional, educational (attention deficit disorder, hyperactivity, all of which we will cover in Chapter 12, "Learning Disabilities"), or physiological. You need to analyze the symptoms, talk to teachers, and develop a plan of action. If your child has an attention problem, oftentimes mild medication will put him back on track. If there is a deep-seated emotional problem, counseling may be the way to go. Or, if your child just does not seem interested in school, you need to spend more time at home stressing the importance of academics (see Chapter 2, "How to Create an Academic Environment at Home").

It is never too late to switch back into honors classes, despite what a school may tell you. If this means that your child has to drop back to regular classes for a time, then so be it. He can always pick up the ball later. Having said this, it is much easier to catch up at the middle school level than at the high school level. If your child is in tenth grade taking precalculus and drops back to trigonometry, it may be impossible without doing extensive summer work to complete advanced-level calculus in high school if that is indeed the goal.

I mention the summer option because a variety of high schools provide excellent academic course work during the summers, all of which allow a child to make up for lost time academically. I will discuss these programs in more depth in Chapter 16, "What to Do during the Summer."

Is It Better to Get Higher Grades in Regular Classes or Lower Grades in Honors Classes?

When I worked in admissions, the question I heard most from high school parents was, "Is it better for my child to get a B in an honors or AP class or an A in a regular class?" My answer was always neither—it is better to get an A in the honors/AP class. While it may sound harsh, there is more than a grain of truth in this response. Parents were asking this question with the idea of sending their children to a very highly selective school. The competition is so tough to get into these schools that virtually everyone who applies is taking all honors or AP courses. So even if you have straight A's but all your classes are regular level, the harsh truth is that you will not even be in the ballpark for consideration. In schools that don't weight grades, the mere rank of valedictorian means nothing to top schools if they can see that the level of course work was not high.

If the child shies away from challenging classes, the most selective colleges won't really care if he has a perfect 4.0 GPA because they consider grades only relative to the level of course difficulty. Therefore, students who take cushy electives or padded courses simply to boost their GPAs will in no way benefit in admission to top colleges. On the other hand, if the child takes AP courses but receives C's and B's in all of them, clearly he has shown that he is not at the top of his class. Ultimately, it is the students who do very well in terms of grades and who are in the most challenging courses who will gain admission to the most selective colleges.

So when looking toward the most selective schools, it always pays to take the most challenging high school course load that you can. However, universities do want to see students who follow their true interests, so in a school that offers AP courses, it would be perfectly okay for a strong humanities student to be taking AP English, AP Spanish, AP science, AP studio art, but regular-level math. Clearly, this student has selected a challenging senior course load, but since he is not interested in math, he has chosen to take this class at the regular level.

By the same token, a strong science or math student might be taking AP calculus (BC level), AP biology, AP chemistry, and AP economics, but standard-level English. Again, this course selection would make sense given the student's interest in math and science, since the two higher-level science classes make for a very challenging year.

This is a dramatic change from a few years ago, when the Ivies and like schools were looking for straight-A students who were well rounded academically and extracurricularly. Now they would much rather have superstars who excel in a few specific areas because ultimately those students are more interesting and bring more talent to their college class.

For example, a good friend of mine was an outstanding bass clarinet player. Although she was by no means a straight-A student and her standardized test scores were not sky high, she was accepted at Yale University because she had dedicated countless hours of practice to reach this level and they realized that ultimately she was more interesting than some student who studied six hours a day and got straight A's. She brought depth, national and international competition experience, her musical talents, and a good work ethic to the school, skills that not every applicant had to offer.

All this is to say that at the high school level you do want to take a challenging class load if you are interested in applying to competitive colleges, but within that general schema, feel free to follow your real academic interests. Don't get forced into a pattern of doing what you think colleges want, because, nine times out of ten, you will be wrong.

What if My Child Is Not Applying to the Most Selective Schools?

Even if you are not applying to top-tier schools, all colleges take into account the level of course difficulty, so if you are talented or interested in a certain area, by all means take the advanced-level course in that field. Many high school students don't realize that by doing well on AP or IB tests, they can save thousands of dollars by getting college credit for this course work. Check college catalogs to see how much credit each college gives for advanced course work.

Where I attended college, if you had three credits coming into school from either AP or IB tests (you usually needed to get a 5/5 on the AP test or a 6 or 7/7 on the IB test), you could take an extra trimester off, thereby saving in the neighborhood of $10,000—nothing to sneeze at!

Though at the middle school level it is sometimes better to drop back to the regular level in some areas, by the time high school rolls around, it is almost always better to struggle a bit in an advanced course than to breeze by in an easy course. Let this be your guiding philosophy in the question of honors versus non-honors classes.

Chapter 12

Learning Disabilities: What Are They and How Do I Know My Child Has One?

"Learning disability" is not a synonym for "unintelligent." In fact, many people you would not normally associate with disabilities suffered from these disorders:[1]

Winston Churchill: Reading problems
Pablo Picasso: Couldn't concentrate and drew pictures all the time in class
Leonardo da Vinci: Had many different LDs, and his teachers thought he was unmotivated
Cher: Had trouble learning how to read
Woodrow Wilson: Poor student
Thomas Edison: Memory problems
Albert Einstein: Expressive language disorder
John Lennon: Written language disorder

What Is a Learning Disability?

A learning disability is a disorder in one or more of the basic psychological processes that underlie learning such subjects as

---

[1]*Keeping a Head in School: A Student's Book about Learning Abilities and Learning Disorders.* Mel Levine. EPS: Cambridge, 1990, p. 257.

speech and language, reading, spelling, or arithmetic. Learning disabilities are not due to emotional problems, mental retardation, or psychological problems. A learning disorder is a problem that does not necessarily show up on standardized tests like the SSAT or the ERBs. A student is considered learning disabled if he has one or more weak brain functions that cause him to do poorly. Sometimes learning problems are referred to as SLDs, which stands for "specific learning disabilities." For ease of reference only, I will generally refer to learning disabilities in this chapter as LDs. One common example of an LD is dyslexia.

There are, depending on how one breaks them down, six main areas where someone can have a learning disability:

1. Reading comprehension
2 Mathematics calculation
3. Math reasoning (problem solving)
4. Oral expression (speaking)
5. Listening comprehension (understanding)
6. Written expression[2]

Attention Deficit Disorder: A Separate Category

In addition to these areas, there is also a separate area (i.e., it is not a "learning disability" at all; it is a separate disorder altogether) called attention deficit disorder (ADD) or attention deficit with hyperactivity disorder (ADHD). As the name indicates, this disorder affects the student's ability to focus on what is being talked about in class. Note that not all students who have ADD have the hyperactivity aspect of the disorder, so it can be hard to identify.

Just because a student has one or more of the above six dis-

---

[2]*Many Ways to Learn: Young People's Guide to Learning Disabilities.* Judith Stern, Uzi Ben Ami. Magination Press: N.Y., 1996.

orders does not automatically mean he also has ADD, but these two areas are co-morbid, meaning that a student with an LD is much more likely also to be ADD than is a student with no LD.

Does It Mean My Child Is of Low Intelligence if He Has an LD?

It is important to note that learning disorders or disabilities are *not* related or correlated to intelligence. In other words, there are students with LDs who are very intelligent, just as there are students with LDs who are not very intelligent. Therefore, it is not fair for one student to call another student with a learning disorder stupid, because there is no relation between the student's intelligence level and whatever his particular disorder may be.

I think this point cannot be overemphasized, especially for parents, who often are reluctant to get their children tested for LDs because they think they will be stigmatized forever. This is just not the case; you will be doing your child a favor to get his LD diagnosed because otherwise he will assume he is not smart when, in fact, he probably is having a very specific problem that can be addressed once it is identified. The real stigma develops for students who are doing poorly in their classes and have done so for as long as they have been in school. Their classmates may think they *are* stupid when they simply may be quite bright with a very specific learning disorder.

How Can You Tell if Your Child Has an LD or Is ADD or ADHD?

If a student has great difficulty learning a school subject even though his intelligence is average or above, he may have an

LD. In the United States, more than 2 million children have some form of LD.

First, let's look at ADD and ADHD separately because sometimes these disorders are more obvious to spot than learning disabilities in particular areas. Here are some of the classic symptoms:

1. Distractibility
2. Impulsiveness
3. Restlessness
4. Disorganization
5. Poor memory
6. Short attention span
7. Short temper
8. Uncontrollable anger
9. Aggressiveness
10. Lack of self-control
11. Stubbornness[3]

If you see some combination of the above symptoms, you want to get your child tested by a professional so you can begin to understand the problem and treat it. I've talked to lots of parents who think that ADD is not a real problem. Their comments usually go something like this: "I mean, when I was in school, we just called them stupid, or nonattentive, but that's because they were lazy and didn't want to do well in school. Besides, they'll grow out of it."

Unfortunately, it's not that easy. While children can grow out of ADD, that fact will not be much help to them in school. If you want to know what it feels like to be ADD, imagine flipping among twenty different TV stations and trying to put together a common narrative. Children with ADD cannot sort different signals, so they cannot listen to the teacher over the

---

[3]*A Parent's Guide to Common and Uncommon School Problems*. David A. Gross. Pia Press, 1989.

other distractions that may be present, like the dog barking outside, another student chewing gum or talking, a paper rustling, the sound of children in the hall, a pencil tapping— you get the idea. These signals all get processed at the same time so that the teacher's lesson does not stand out among the other sounds.

Contrary to what these parents may have thought, ADD is scientifically proven to be a real disorder. Scientists have studied brain functions of children with ADD, and there is a concrete difference in how information is processed by the brain. It is not a made-up disorder. Finally, children with ADD often are trying their hardest and tend not to be lazy; they just don't know how to go about sifting all the signals they are getting. It is unfair to assume that a student with ADD is stupid or lazy, because, more likely than not, he is neither. Besides, if a parent is going to assume that a child is stupid or lazy, that kind of thinking does not lend itself to a productive solution to the problem.

What are some of the common characteristics of learning disorders (as opposed to ADD or ADHD)?

1. Students are receiving poor grades in school.
2. Students have average to high IQs but are not receiving good grades.
3. Students spend hours doing homework but still don't do well.
4. Students have an aversion to reading.
5. Students are constantly getting in trouble in school.
6. Students get frustrated easily and tend to give up when doing homework assignments.
7. Students seem to understand the material but just can't seem to do well on tests or quizzes.
8. Students run out of time on tests or quizzes.
9. Students have low self-esteem.
10. Students seem to be unable to learn a foreign language.
11. Students have illegible handwriting and/or poor motor skills.

Oftentimes parents are the last to notice, or at least the last to acknowledge, that a child may have an LD. Therefore, teachers often force the issue. If you meet with your child's teachers and they indicate that they think there is a chance that your child has an LD, get the child evaluated! As a popular maxim for LD specialists says, "The only consistent thing about LDs is their inconsistency," meaning that a child may do fine in one area one year and then drop to a failing grade the next, and then rise the next year, and so on.

The more you can pinpoint what the problem is (or whether there is a problem at all), the more you can face it and develop a solution. The worst thing to do, especially during the difficult middle school years, is to let a problem go unchecked. It will only reinforce to your child that he is indeed not as bright as other kids and cannot succeed in school. This having been said, what are the tests and what do they show?

Testing

In public schools, to qualify for LD programs, most schools require evidence of a two-year discrepancy between expected performance and actual performance (IQ). This of course refers to when the student is two years below where he should be, not if he's two years ahead of where he should be because of high IQ.

It's useful to know that all public high schools have a booklet for parents on every exceptionality that tells them their rights, the definitions, and the order of steps that you go through the process. This booklet is the schools' adaptation of national law 94-142, which covers students from ages three to twenty-one, and it is the first place for parents to begin.

As early as pre-kindergarten, parents have the right to have their children assessed by the district. Your first recourse should be to use the school's resources for testing. However, if you are dissatisfied with the school's report, you have a right to a private evaluation (from a licensed professional) that the public school may be required to pay for.

What Does a Good Evaluation Consist of?

When a student gets "evaluated," it means he gets tested by one or more experts in learning disorders.[4] The first part of an evaluation is the administration of an IQ test. The most common is the WISC (Wechsler Intelligence Test for Children 5–16), followed by the Stanford-Binet. On the IQ scale, 100 is average, 85–100 is low-average, 100–115 is high-average, 115–130 is above average, and 130 is superior (and often the cutoff for inclusion in "gifted programs"). Both the WISC and the Stanford-Binet are scored the same way, but the WISC is the test given most often because it is more current for norming and prediction of academic performance. It measures how well a student has learned what he knows and how quickly he has learned knowledge as compared to others.

The report should also include an examination of the left and right areas of the brain and discrepancies between the two. The right brain is generally considered the creative, abstract, and artistic side, while the left brain handles many concrete functions like reading and writing. This assessment can be even more important than the total IQ scores in determining LDs.

If a student's IQ turns out to be 120, that's the expected score for achievement testing. If it then turns out that the achievement testing shows a two-year discrepancy, this would be the sign of an LD. There exists also a special category for "gifted LD" students, which means that their grade-level performance may be adequate but still way below their potential. These students would not qualify for traditional LD accommodations, but it is still useful to know where your child falls

---

[4]*Keeping a Head in School: A Student's Book about Learning Abilities and Learning Disorders.* Mel Levine. EPS: Cambridge, 1990.

in terms of the evaluation. In the private sector, there are many specialists who help these gifted LD students achieve up to their potential whether they are in private or public school.

The testing should also include any specific modalities (auditory, visual) that are missing or deficient, as well as some emotional tests. Even in the event that no LDs are detected, a good report will also include a full evaluation of the student's strengths and weaknesses. This analysis can be very helpful to parents who are trying to see why their child is struggling in school. The people administering the test should either rule out ADD or include it. Although not all testers abide by the same rule, to be considered ADD, the student should be in the bottom 5 percent in terms of impulsiveness, concentration, and distractibility.

Testing can be done as early as three years of age. Standard testing costs $1,000 to $2,000. If you don't have the money, the public school is required to pay or do the testing itself. If the student is in private school, parents should go to the home district (where they live) to have the child tested in the local school.

Once testing is requested, it must take place in a "reasonable period of time" (i.e., less than sixty days). It is illegal for the school to let a major period of time like two years go by without complying with the request.

What Are Some Tips for Parents on How to Be an Advocate for Your Child?

1. Keep a telephone log in a folder with names and dates of whom you spoke to and when. For example: *3/12/99 2:40 p.m. Spoke to Mrs. Jones, Jake's sixth-grade teacher, about why he was failing English. She recommended getting Jake tested for an LD because of poor spelling.*
2. Notify anyone of any decision you make *in writing*—for example, the principal, or the superintendent. Send copies

to lots of people, using sentences like "We are looking forward to setting the schedule for the testing." In this way, school officials are more likely to act upon what you have requested because it will make them look foolish if they don't.

3. You have the right to sit down at a case conference after the test is given with the people who gave the test and have it interpreted for you. You should tape this! Tell the specialists ahead of time that you want to tape the presentation. It is a good idea to have your child present at these conversations. You have the right to take that report to a private examiner and get a second opinion. There are parent advocates or psychologists who can go with you as your representative.

4. Ask if your child is eligible for special programs.

5. Follow up! At the second or third meeting, ask specific questions like "Where are we putting him, for how long, and how will we monitor his progress?" and "What are the goals we are trying to achieve?"

6. Be sure that you agree mutually upon the plan—if you have any problems, keep meeting until all parties reach an agreement.

7. Ask the school for all its written information on the subject of services for exceptional students. I have a brochure in front of me from the Broward Board of Education called, *Parent Primer: An Introduction to ESE Services for Parents of Exceptional Students.* By law, schools must have this information in writing for parents.

8. Teach your child what you are doing so he learns to be his own advocate. In the long run, those students with LDs who are the most successful are those who learn how to ask for what they need in terms of accommodations. High school students should actually sit in on parent-school meetings when the individual program is being discussed.

In this section, I address techniques that students can use to show teachers they are trying. Please have your children read this section with you. Students should:

1. Act friendly and not blame teachers for any difficulties they are having.
2. Try to talk to teachers in private so they can speak freely.
3. Share their true feelings; if something the teacher did bothered them, it's likely he did not even realize it. Keep open the lines of communication.
4. Take the initiative; if the student is having problems in a subject, it is *his* job to make an appointment to see the teacher.
5. Try to let the teacher know how they are working to help their LD and be sure to let him know exactly what the problem is and how the teacher can help.
6. Do more than they are asked to do every once in a while, in order to show that they are really trying.
7. Let the teacher know when they think he has done a really good job of teaching them—students have the power to reinforce the teacher's methods. Remember, many teachers have no special training in helping LD kids.
8. If they want, write a note to the teacher, especially if it's hard for them to talk to him directly.
9. Encourage their parents to go to meetings at school.
10. Try not to be rude or irritating in class.[5]

Here are some ways a student can make accommodations for himself:

1. Use a word processor for writing reports to take advantage of spell-check functions.
2. Use a calculator in math if the teacher allows it.
3. Before writing a report, dictate ideas into a tape recorder.

---

[5]*Keeping a Head in School: A Student's Book about Learning Abilities and Learning Disorders.* Mel Levine. EPS: Cambridge, 1990, p. 266.

4. Sit in the front and close to the teacher in order to focus better.

5. Make diagrams and charts while reading.[6]

If Your Child Is Diagnosed by a Private Specialist, Should You Inform the School?

As a parent, you should feel free to have your children evaluated without the fear that you will have to hand over the results. In fact, the only reason you would make the information "public" would be to share it with a public school so your children can qualify for a specific program at the school. Only in extreme cases (i.e., your child has been failing all subjects repeatedly and you refuse to cooperate) can the school ask for compliance via the "due process" clause to share evaluation results or to have the child evaluated by its own experts. Other than that, you are under no obligation to pass the evaluation along unless you want to.

Should You Let Your Child Take Untimed SAT I and SAT II Tests if He Qualifies? How Do Colleges Look at Untimed Testing?

There have been many articles regarding the abuse of the system in terms of non-LD students requesting untimed testing. In New York City, wealthy parents were paying specialists to testify to their child's LD so in effect he would have unlimited, or at least extra, time on the SATs. Since then, the Educational Testing Service has made the process much more stringent. You have to have a full testing report done, not just a note from a doctor.

---

[6]*Keeping a Head in School: A Student's Book about Learning Abilities and Learning Disorders.* Mel Levine. EPS: Cambridge, 1990, pp. 270–71.

It is a shame that parents even feel in the first place that they can try to "pass off" their children as LD just to give them an unfair advantage on standardized tests. I can't think of a more subversive way to undermine a system that has been modified to help genuinely LD students achieve closer to their "true" score on the SAT I.

Of course it is perfectly legitimate to take the untimed version of the SAT I if your child qualifies. Keep in mind that when the test results are reported to colleges, they will be instantly aware that he took the untimed tests because of how the scores are reported. So if you are trying to hide the fact that your child took the untimed test, it is impossible.

The overall point is that if your child is legitimately LD, there is no reason at all to hide the fact that he is taking the untimed test. Quite the opposite: He will want to explain somewhere on his college applications what kind of LD he has and what he has done to accommodate it. Being honest will in no way hurt his chances of getting into college. However, not showing any evidence of having an LD and somehow being allowed to take the untimed test might make colleges think that he is simply trying to abuse the system.

Remember: From the colleges' point of view, they are aware that SLDs do not correspond directly to intelligence. They are searching for students who love learning and show a certain degree of intellectual spark. If they know a student is LD, they will still judge him using the same criteria they would use in judging any student: How has the student done in his classes? Where does he rank in his high school? How well has he scored on national tests like the SAT I and SAT II? If they know that a student, despite a severe learning disability, has worked so hard to overcome the problem that he graduated near the top of his class and teachers say he loves learning, they can see that the student has learned to overcome the LD. Therefore, the college is not taking a risk because the child has a proven track record of success.

As you can see in the case above, colleges would tend to accord an even higher respect knowing that the student had to overcome a great deal to get as far as he did. So students do not need to feel like they should hide their LD; quite to the contrary, it is better to disclose fully and then let colleges judge you on your real intellectual merits. If you are learning disabled and you know that taking the untimed test would increase your score, take the test untimed!

Asking for Accommodations

You as the parent have the right to ask for "reasonable" accommodations if your child is ADD or ADHD. Obviously, the definition of *reasonable* is not as straightforward as it would appear. I have reproduced below a note from a typical school showing how schools have to support the American Disabilities Act.

American Disabilities Act (ADA) Policy

"Students seeking reasonable accommodations for a disability are required to submit to the ADA Coordinator appropriate written documentation indicating that the disability substantially limits some major life activity, including learning. Our school follows the policies outlined by C.H.A.D.D., the College Board, and the Educational Testing Service to assure that documentation is suitable to verify eligibility and support the request for accommodations from middle school, high school and the college testing/admissions process.

"Designation as an individual with a disability does not afford any individual automatic access to accommodations. Nor does prior designation by another party or agency automatically qualify the individual for privileges as a disabled individual at the school. Our school has established these guidelines in the interest of meeting the diverse needs of the population of students with learning disabilities enrolled here."

Chapter 13

Other Hindrances to Learning

What can you do if you think something is interfering with your child's learning in school? First, you need to assess the problem. One rule of thumb for parents to keep in mind: Always be sure to rule out hearing or eyesight as a problem before getting a full evaluation. Although it may sound obvious, you'd be surprised how often the most obvious problems are overlooked while much money and time are spent trying to solve problems that aren't there.

How Can You Judge When Something Is Interfering?

Let me recount a true story about a woman in New York City whose child, normally an A student, suddenly started getting D's and F's in French class. Even though her child was only in seventh grade, she found it unusual that he would be doing so poorly in a subject he liked so much. She decided, almost on a whim, to spend a day going to school with her son to observe the classes. What she noticed was that during the period her son had French, there was a very loud construction project going on outside the window that made it very hard for some of the students to hear what the teacher was saying. Since much of the grade was determined by oral comprehension, her son was doing poorly because he had trouble hearing.

Though this might sound obvious, the noise was not loud enough that the students made a conscious note of it, and some were sitting farther away. The teacher, though she found it annoying, was doing her best to shout over the racket and assumed that everyone could hear her. Once the parent contacted the school administration, the construction schedule was changed so as not to interfere with academic classes. The moral of the story is, sometimes the only way to assess the conditions in the classroom is to make an appearance in the classroom yourself so you can evaluate the ambient circumstances.

What Can You Do if Your Child Is Physically or Psychologically Threatened at School?

One mother recently recounted to me that she almost pulled her son out of public school because he was afraid to use the bathrooms since he was getting beaten up and teased every time he went in. Her son didn't even want to tell his mother what the problem was, but when his grades started dropping and she noticed that he would run for the bathroom as soon as he got home, she finally got the truth from him.

No doubt, the quickest solution is to change schools, but in many cases this is not possible, and certainly it is not the most desirable solution. You always want to try to work within the system first to resolve problems once you can identify them. In this case, the problem was that many children, not just this one boy, were being terrorized in the bathrooms. She got together with a group of parents and made an appointment with the school principal.

Once the school administration heard about the problem, they quickly investigated, found out who the ringleaders were, and suspended most of them and expelled the major ringleader. Then they assigned faculty to the bathrooms each and every period to make random passes so that students always knew that any minute a faculty member would be walking in. Within the week, there were no problems with the bathrooms and students could once again use them without living in fear of being terrorized.

The plan of action worked because it followed these steps:

1. The parent talked to other parents and realized the problem was widespread.
2. She took the problem right to the top administrator, who could not ignore the problem without looking ineffectual.
3. She pointed out that the behavior was interfering with learning because the students could not concentrate on their classes if they were in constant fear.
4. She gave the administration a chance to formulate a plan.

Let's say the problem was specific to your child, i.e., students were picking on him because he was tall, or short, or overweight, or whatever. You need to make the right person aware of the problem. First you need to find out who is intimidating your child and whether that same person is bothering others as well. Then you need to talk to the school counselor, being sure to document, or take notes on, all conversations you have with school officials. Note down the date and time and exactly whom you spoke to. If they know you are keeping track, administrators are more likely to take action so it doesn't look like they are not doing their job.

In this case, you might want to start with the counselor and let him know that "Jake" is constantly teasing your child. The counselor can then decide what action to take. He might want to talk directly to Jake, or have the teacher take him aside. The counselor might decide that the problem is so widespread that the school needs to have an assembly on treating others well. In short, you want to push the school into acknowledging the problem and taking positive steps to resolve it.

If you are not satisfied with the first person who has dealt with the problem, you need to keep taking it to the next level: the vice principal, the principal, the superintendent of schools—whatever it takes. Be sure to have a typed list of whom you have spoken to and when, so when you take the problem to the next level, you can show who is at fault for not resolving the problem. You'll find that most schools want to work with you to resolve these problems because they share an interest in not having anything interfere with the learning process.

In rare cases, you may find that the problem lies with your child, not with other children. Let's say that your child is so shy that he cannot talk in class and cannot get up enough courage even to raise his hand. He may feel like others are picking on him, but the truth may be that he is so introverted he is incapable of reaching out to others and making friends.

After you speak to the school counselor, it might be necessary to seek an outside counselor or therapist to help your child get over this problem. In a case like this it is not the school's responsibility to resolve the problem, since the child has some kind of emotional issue. Still, your first recourse should always be to go through the school and seek advice, but keep in mind that ultimately you may have to step in and solve the problem yourself. One side benefit of going through the "proper" channels is that you are teaching (by modeling) your children conflict-resolution skills that will be useful their whole lives.

What Can You Do About Late Lunches and Other "Set" School Functions?

One parent I spoke to this year was concerned that her child was not doing well in all her classes. When she compared grades by class, she noticed that her daughter's lowest grades were in the classes she had right before lunch. As it turned out, her daughter didn't eat breakfast and the school had assigned her the last lunch period, at 1:20 P.M. Once the mother figured out that her child was running out of brain energy, she started not only making her daughter eat breakfast, but she also sent her to school with a light snack so that she could eat something when she began to run out of energy.

In this case, the girl's schedule was so tight that she could not change the lunch period, but another possible solution was to ask the school to try to switch the schedule around. Again, the same lesson applies. You as a parent need to:

1. Assess the problem
2. Come up with a plan of action
3. Document all calls and school contacts
4. Make suggestions for what you would like to see happen if the school runs out of ideas
5. Assess your own child: Perhaps he is the problem

With set functions like lunches, study halls, and music lessons, you need to be in contact with the school to make a complaint or suggest an alternative plan if you see that something in the schedule is interfering with your child's ability to learn. You do not have to accept "fixed" items in the schedule automatically. Schools have to be flexible too. Always start on a positive note when talking to people at the school. Give them the benefit of the doubt that they too want to work with you to resolve the problem. Also, get an early start: Try to resolve these potential problems in the last two weeks of summer vacation when most teachers (or at least administrators) are at work and are not as busy as they are during the school year. It's much easier to nip the problem in the bud (i.e., when a preliminary schedule is ready) than it is to solve a scheduling problem midway through the year.

There is no point in antagonizing the school. Think of your relationship as a real partnership: The school wants the best for your child and you want to help the school help your child! Many schools are so big or so poorly run that they are honestly not aware of many problems. Think of it as your job, as an advocate for your child, to question the school, and to bring problems to the school's attention so it can do something toward solving them with you. In many cases, you are helping other students besides your own children.

Chapter 14

What Should You Do When Your Child Has a Conflict with a Specific Teacher?

While I don't want to sidestep the issue, keep in mind that more times than not, particularly at the middle school level, children are not the most reliable judge of teachers. Let's look at two contrasting middle school-teacher types. Teacher number one is an experienced female teacher, middle-aged, who is very demanding. Although she is very fair, she holds her students to high standards, has a very defined course outline, and always does an excellent job preparing the students for higher-level writing and thinking. However, she does not accept late assignments. Teacher number two is a young man, just out of college, who is a little immature and spends a good deal of time trying to impress the children and become their friend. They all think he's cool, and they feel they can talk to him about their problems and fears, but he's slacking off in terms of lesson preparation and concrete homework.

Probably 95 percent of any middle school sampling would say that teacher number two is a cool guy and they love his class, while just as many would complain that teacher number one is mean, not "fun," and doesn't seem to care about them. Most would rank number two well above number one.

I'm sure that by now you can see the problem: Middle school students judge teachers primarily on a personal level and tend to be swayed very much by their peer group. Not that personality is not crucial for a middle school teacher. I would agree that you don't want an old, stodgy teacher who simply lectures young students endlessly. Middle school teachers must be able to motivate, entertain, and cover content area, and that's why it's truly difficult to find excellent middle school teachers. There is a difference, though, between a teacher who is demanding (i.e., not accepting late homework or reports) and one who is unreasonable (i.e., says she will not count the quiz but then does anyway).

In either case, the message to get across to your children is that they can learn something from any teacher if they make an effort. You do not want to teach your children that the minute they don't think a teacher is great, you will run into school and change it. Whether you are talking about middle school, high school, college, or graduate school, there are an infinite combination of teaching styles and techniques. Some teachers are truly inspiring, some make up for what they lack in personal dynamism in terms of great content and knowledge of subject, some are truly mediocre and should not be teaching. My two points are that (a) your child will not always be the most reliable judge, and (b) your child cannot always count on getting an ideal teacher. Therefore, it's necessary for your child to learn to make the best of the occasional mediocre teacher.

If you have any doubt, take a moment now and think of a teacher from either your middle school or your high school whom you didn't like at the time but came to appreciate years later because you learned so much. I remember a sixth-grade science teacher who almost all my friends thought was weird and kind of boring. I might have thought so for a while too, but one day he caught me reading a book on astronomy and spent an hour sharing his knowledge of the stars with me and comparing notes. From that day on, I started appreciating his knowledge much more and really listening when he taught. Though he wasn't a great entertainer, he was so knowledgeable that his class soon became my favorite. I had another teacher who terrified me—I thought anyone who taught by fear could not be good. Although I wouldn't choose to sit through his class a second time, he taught me a lot and I learned how to deal with a very high-pressure class, which came in handy when college rolled around.

If I had just judged these teachers quickly, as my peers did, I would have spent most of the year making fun of them and not learning as much as I could have by listening and giving them the benefit of the doubt. Remember, no one goes into teaching because of the money.

To restate an important point: Always take what your children say with a grain of salt. However, do take the time to listen to what they say, because sometimes students are the most sensitive and tuned in to legitimate problems with a teacher. For example, in one school where I worked we had a middle school teacher who came across as a real dynamo. He was young and handsome, and everyone seemed fond of him.

Within a few weeks' time, though, we noticed a trend of students starting to feel uncomfortable in his class and suddenly deciding they didn't like him as much. After speaking with several students, it turned out that he was putting his hands on their shoulders and touching them in other small but noticeable ways. He also was making sexually inappropriate comments in class. After an administrator overheard some of the things he was saying, we investigated and found that, in fact, he was making the students uncomfortable and he was saying inappropriate things that bordered on harassment.

In this case, we as a school listened to the students' complaints and followed up. The complaints turned out to be very valid, and we let the teacher go.

By now, another point should be obvious: If your child is going to complain about a teacher, force your child to be specific and give examples. "I think Ms. Fichter is a jerk" is not a helpful comment, whereas "I think Ms. Fichter is a jerk because she hit a kid with a baseball bat" is—well, you get the idea.

What to Do if Your Child Says He *Hates* His Teacher or Thinks the Teacher Is Picking on Him

Let's formalize the steps so you can plan out your actions.

1. Force your child to be specific: Write down all the things he complains about.
2. Study the list. What is your first reaction? Are the complaints superficial or petty? Do they sound like excuses for not doing well in class?
3. Consider how your child is doing in that class. Oftentimes when a child gets a low grade, he may try to blame the teacher rather than take responsibility.
4. Talk to other parents and students in the class. There's no place like the carpool crowd to get the scoop! See if your child's complaints are isolated or generally agreed upon.

The Chain of Command

Let's say you followed all the above steps and you are convinced there is a problem in the class. If the problem is relatively minor (meaning that it would make sense to see the teacher first), here is one model of the steps you should take:

1. Make an appointment with the teacher if you feel comfortable talking directly to him. If not, make an appointment with an administrator. Express your concerns in a constructive way, being sure to give the teacher the benefit of the doubt until proven guilty. For example, "For some reason, Janet feels that you don't value her opinion and don't call on her in class even when she raises her hand.

We know she is quiet, but she loves reading and would like to be involved more in your class. We're concerned that her lack of participation is hurting her grade."

This kind of approach is productive because it doesn't put the teacher immediately on the defensive. You are just saying how your child *feels,* not accusing the teacher of anything. You are also acknowledging your child's own weaknesses rather than insisting that your child is a genius and that she can't be wrong. In effect, you are giving the teacher a graceful way out rather than backing him into a corner. The teacher can at least express his point of view without feeling threatened.

If done well, a frank talk with the teacher will clear the air and make the teacher aware of a behavior or problem that he probably was not previously aware of. Most teachers very much appreciate parents who will work with them. Maybe you informed him that your daughter was going through a rough time since her grandmother died and that's why she was acting out.

By being nonconfrontational and acknowledging that your own child is not an angel, you will win a teacher over and create a solid working relationship. Creating this relationship benefits both you and your child. In effect, it opens up a line of communication. You might say something like, "Please call me immediately if Susan responds rudely in class again because we are trying to work with her on this problem."

2. If the problem is too personal (i.e., sexual harassment or anything you could not say directly to the teacher), make an appointment with the head of the department and discuss your concerns, following the above model for the teacher. Take notes and have all your own points written down before you go in.

3. If there is no department head or you don't have faith in him, move up the administrative ladder, to the assistant principal and then the principal.

How to Establish a Paper Trail

Every time you meet with a school official either on the phone or in person, take notes and list the time and the date of every conversation. If you are meeting in person, I wouldn't suggest taking notes right in front of the official because it may make him uncomfortable and less likely to be direct with you. However, as soon as you leave, jot down as many points as you can remember.

If you do not feel satisfied that the problem is being resolved, type up all the notes so you will have a record of all the people with whom you have tried to resolve it. If you send a letter or any official correspondence to the school or a teacher, be sure to keep photocopies for your records. In the event that a problem escalates, you will need as much written proof as you can gather about what positive steps you have taken and how the school has dropped the ball. Even in the extreme case in which a serious complaint might make it to court, at least if you have a written record you will be able to document the fact that you took positive steps to resolve the problem and it was the school that did not comply.

Will It Hurt My Child's Grade if I Go to the Teacher Directly?

If you follow the instructions above for talking directly to the teacher and expressing your concerns without being confrontational, you will in no way hurt your child's grade. In fact, contrary to what children say ("I can't believe he gave me a C"), grades are earned by your children. Anytime a student tells me that he can't believe I gave him a certain grade on a test, I have to point out that I only gave the test—he earned the grade.

I think as long as you are respectful and constructive when

talking to your children's teachers, you are only opening up a line of communication, not hurting their grade. As I explained before, much of the time the teacher will learn something about the child or the family that will actually make the teacher appreciate more what that child may be going through.

Just recently, a mother of a child in my English class came into school to let me know that her child's recent low grades were not due to laziness, but rather to the fact that her bat mitzvah was just around the corner and the preparation was taking up all her time. Once I knew that and could understand the problem, I didn't have to start building up anger or resentment that the student was blowing off my class to spend time with friends.

In a case like this, you can see that the fact that you included the teacher in the "loop" has no adverse effect whatsoever on your child's grades.

Two constructive steps you can take are:

1. Keep track of your child's grades in every class so that you have a clear record that you can compare with the teacher's records if there is a discrepancy.
2. Make it a point to ask the teacher what the distribution of grades was in your child's class. For example, if 75 percent of the grades were A's and 25 percent were F's and there was no grade in between, you'd have some idea that the grading might not be fair or accurate. Knowing this distribution will help you when you speak to teachers.

In the very rare and unlikely event that a teacher would get so angry at parents that he would even think of altering a student's grade, you can protect yourself by keeping a paper trail. If your child had an A average and because of a personal conflict between the teacher and you or your child that you had fully documented, the teacher decided to give a C–, you would be able to go to the next administrative level to resolve the problem. In cases where documentation is thorough, schools usually do the right thing and will change a grade if the teacher was proven to be unfair.

How to Improve the Teacher-Student Relationship

Now that we've focused only on problems, let's take a step back and look at how to create a positive relationship with your child's teachers.

First, go to parent-teacher night and judge teachers for yourself. Now that you have heard your child either complain or praise a teacher for months, you'll have the chance to judge for yourself, since teachers generally make a brief presentation for parents. If the teacher bores you to death, chances are he bores your child to death, too. If he seems energetic and smart, he probably is energetic and smart. Ask yourself the following questions:

1. Does he know his subject matter?
2. Does he explain things in a clear way?
3. Is it easy to understand his voice and inflection?
4. Does he have an easygoing manner?
5. Does he come across as organized?
6. Does he have a coherent explanation of the course of study?
7. Has he explained exactly what criteria he uses to calculate your child's grade?
8. Does he seem able to control a class of active children?
9. Does he do a good job answering parents' questions and concerns?
10. *Very important:* Does he make himself available for extra help either during school or after school?

These are the kinds of questions you should write down and keep track of. Then match your impressions with those of your child. If you say Mrs. So-and-So seems to be brilliant and entertaining, and your son says "She's my favorite teacher ever," you know that you see eye to eye.

After you have heard the teachers talk, be sure to go up and introduce yourself so they can match the student with the parent. If you know your child is having difficulty in the class, say something like "Hi, Mr. Pavlica, nice to meet you. I'm Joey's mom and I'd like to meet with you soon to see how we can help Joey do better in your class."

Without being accusatory or aggressive, you have expressed your interest in supporting the teacher and working with him to find out where the problem lies. The hardest thing to face as a parent is that you cannot always believe your child. I have seen too many cases of children who become experts at deceiving their parents. Low grades or weak tests are never their fault or their responsibility. Though sometimes your child will be right, it teaches a better life lesson if you first assume the teacher is right and then work with that teacher to see what needs to be done.

No matter how much you love your children, they are not always right about teachers and often do not really know why they are not doing well in a class. It might take a teacher to tell you that she assigns fifteen vocabulary words a week and your son is not putting in the time to make index cards like most other students in the class. In this example, rather than scold your child, you can begin to take positive steps to help him make cards and test him once a week on the words.

E-Mailing Your Child's Teachers

Now that many schools have E-mail for their teachers, establish an E-mail connection with teachers once you have made personal contact. Don't flood teachers with three messages a day, but if you are concerned about a particular issue, drop them an E-mail. Of course phone calls work too, but keep in mind that often it's much quicker to respond to a few parent

E-mails than to spend the day trying to catch up on parent phone calls.

As far as other tips about establishing a relationship, give praise when praise is due. Teaching is a tough profession. The good teachers don't get paid more than the bad ones, and often talented teachers go relatively unrecognized. Call or E-mail just to say that your child loves the class. It just takes one phone call like this to keep a teacher going. Or, if you find a newspaper article or book that you think might interest one of your child's teachers, send it to him either with your child or by mail to the school. Teachers often get so busy that they don't have time to read the paper every day or catch up on all the books they would love to read if they didn't have to grade papers until late on many nights.

In short, do what you can to accord respect to your children's teachers. Remember that in other countries besides the United States (Japan, Germany, China, and scores of others) teachers are regarded with a tremendous amount of respect and are often paid accordingly. Don't develop a reputation as a parent who is constantly complaining about everything and everyone in the school. If you seldom complain, the one time you have a valid complaint, you are much more credible and more likely to be listened to.

How to Request Teacher Recommendations for Other Schools without Offending the Teacher

You don't need to worry that much about offending teachers with such a request. It is routine to ask for a letter of recommendation. You could be moving to a different place or moving because of financial reasons that have nothing to do with the school. If you are requesting these references, you can feel free to tell teachers that you have a particular reason. Don't be needlessly confrontational. Even if you are leaving the school because you think all the teachers are horrible, just say that you are seeking a different type of school experience for your child, or an alternative environment.

How to Supplement a Weak Class at Home without Taking the Heat

If your child has one weak teacher at either the middle school or high school level and you are afraid he will fall behind, you have only three real options.

1. Call the school's registrar or whoever handles schedules and find out if your child's schedule could be changed around without causing too much disruption. If the change means that you'd have to change all your child's other teachers, it's probably not worth it. Or there may not be anyone else who teaches that class at that level. Find out whether or not a change is possible.

2. If it isn't, you should complain in writing to someone that you feel the teacher is not covering the curriculum. Be specific and don't make generalizations that are true only for a small group of children. And, since the teacher will probably be there until at least the end of the year, you need to go to plan B, which is to make sure you take it upon yourself to teach your child at home in that topic or get a tutor.

3. See your child's guidance counselor, whose job it is to make sure your child's schedule runs satisfactorily. The guidance counselor will work in concert with the registrar if changes are approved.

If you know that it is impossible to change your child's schedule, there is no need to get into a big fight with the teacher over his lack of ability to teach a topic. If it happens to be a subject you know about, try to fill in the blanks at home. Let's take a simple example. Your child has an incompetent Spanish teacher and even though this is the second year he has had

Spanish, the teacher has such poor control over the classroom and such poor technique that your child is not learning anything. Even if you don't know any Spanish, you can follow along in the textbook or workbook that your child uses in the class and practice vocabulary and grammar just by assigning work. You'd be surprised how easy to follow many good textbooks are. If you reviewed a chapter on traveling in airports, you could test him on all the vocabulary, read the explanations of grammar, and then do the exercises with him. You could probably even make a quiz or test by following the book.

If it's a subject you really cannot understand at all (let's say math for the sake of argument), it's better to bite the bullet and hire a tutor. If you are trying to save money, hire a student from the local high school, who will probably be better able to follow the curriculum since he went through the same program and will definitely charge less than a "professional" tutor.

By either doing the teaching yourself or hiring a tutor, you are teaching an important lesson to your child: Just because a teacher is bad doesn't mean that you give up and go along with not doing anything. You need to inculcate in your children the desire to make the most of their education and to pursue knowledge even when it's difficult.

Finally, if you are tutoring your child at home, don't reinforce the obvious fact that you are doing this because the teacher is horrible. In fact, it's better not to go along with the adolescent tendency to blame teachers if learning is not taking place. It's far better to teach your children *that they can learn something from everyone* and you hired a tutor so they could learn even more in depth and be better able to succeed the following year, since the curriculum gets harder. Clearly, it's not a good idea for your child to blurt out to the teacher in question that because he's terrible, his parents decided to have him tutored at home. You don't want to jeopardize your child's grade in any way. Be smart and be diplomatic: Your primary concern should be to help your child get by a temporary rough spot by filling in holes in his education. Even the finest schools have the occasional bad teacher, so just assume that your child will have one at some point and try to deal with it in the most practical way possible while keeping a positive attitude.

Chapter 15

Standardized Testing

If you are unfamiliar with standardized testing, learning the different test names and objectives can be intimidating. Even if you have already been through the testing loop with a younger child, be aware that in the last few years there have been major changes to many of the standardized tests, so it is worth revisiting the topic.

The SAT I and PSAT

The SAT I used to be called the Scholastic Aptitude Test, but the College Board of the Educational Testing Service (ETS—we have them to thank for all these tests) changed the name a few years ago to the Scholastic Assessment Test because of the controversy surrounding the term *aptitude*. Now they just admit to "assessing" intelligence rather than determining a student's aptitude. The SAT I is a three-hour test that is split up into a verbal part and a math part. Therefore, students' scores are reported in pairs reflecting their scores on each section.

Why the PSAT Is More Important Than Most People Think

The PSAT is the "preliminary" SAT or the practice version of the real test (though I will emphasize that your children must not slough it off as just practice). It is usually given in the tenth grade, a year before most students take the official PSAT and the actual SAT in eleventh grade. Though many think it's not an important test, I disagree because PSAT scores are usually very indicative of what a student's SAT scores will be. But that's not the main reason why they are important: *The real reason is that the testing people use the PSAT scores to qualify students across the country for National Merit Semi-Finalists and Finalists.* These awards are important both for winning scholarship money and for accolades that colleges will notice.

The main point is that you want to prepare your children to take the PSAT very seriously even though it is only a practice test, and you want to make sure that any preparation is completed well before the fall of eleventh grade, when the test is administered.

Since the test is scored on a scale of 200 to 800 with 500 being the average, an average score would be 500 verbal and 500 math. This score would mean that 50 percent of those who took the test scored higher and 50 percent scored lower than your child.

I don't want to go into all the gory mathematical details, but right around the time the ETS changed the name of the test and the content (the old test used to have antonyms, but now it has more reading comprehension), they also recentered the test.

At the simplest level, all we need to know is that the "average" score used to be in the low 400s for verbal and math. The problem was that since the average was different for each section, a student could not interpret his scores very well because a 430V, 430M did not actually mean that he was the same in both areas, since the average score for each section was different.

Basically, the testing service recentered both the math and the verbal around a 500 average so that 500 is always the median score (half scored higher, half scored lower). What this means for those of you with children who took the old test and younger children who will take the new test is that the scores look higher now. If your older child scored a 750 on the verbal a few years ago, that was a *much* higher score than a 750 verbal now.

It also means that the magic score of 1,400 combined (which used to be considered the standard for getting into highly selective colleges) is now a much more average score. In other words, a 1,400 combined used to be a rare phenomenon, but now the average combined SAT I at the most selective colleges is around a 1,420!

This fact has nothing to do with students being smarter now than they were; it's just easier to get in the 700 range now because of the fairer way scores are distributed. Now the scores come out an almost perfect bell curve, whereas a few years ago, the curve was skewed such that only 1 percent of all students scored in the 700 range in the verbal section.

The Verbal Section

Having said all this, what do these tests really show? The verbal section is a reading test. It does cover vocabulary (mostly in context as opposed to words taken in lists), but no student who is a weak reader will score above a 600 on the verbal score. The best preparation for the verbal test starts as early as elementary school—you need to encourage your children to read, read, and read more. You also, as we have discussed, need to serve as a role model for them so they can see that you read as well.

Along with reading, children need to be picking up vocabulary as well. If the school curriculum is weak in vocabulary, buy an SAT vocabulary book or any school textbook on vocabulary and insist that your children learn ten words a week starting in fifth or sixth grade. If you encourage both active reading and vocabulary acquisition from an early age, you will find that the only preparation necessary for taking both the SAT I and the PSAT is to take one or two practice tests (available in bookstores and directly from ETS) before the test date in order to become so familiar with the format that it is not necessary to waste time reading the directions.

The Math Section

The problem with the math section is that by the time students take the test, many of those who are in advanced math are actually ahead of where they need to be. Ironically, those students in the most advanced math sections are likely to feel that the SAT math is old stuff and they may have already forgotten how to do some of it.

After taking a practice test as a diagnostic, I would go from there to decide how best to prepare for this section. Some students have such a good math curriculum that they score over 700 with little effort. If after taking a practice test the score is under 600, it may be worthwhile either to enroll in an SAT prep course or to hire a private tutor who specializes in this kind of math.

The math section does not really test what a great math student you are; the math is relatively simple and formulaic. I've seen students who are brilliant in math and who score 5 out of 5 on the AP exam in calculus (which I'll explain soon) who do *not* do extremely well on the SAT math section, probably because it is very basic. Therefore, it is definitely worth prepping for.

Unless your children are applying to specialized schools in math or engineering (MIT, RPI), in most cases the verbal score will be the one that colleges (especially liberal arts colleges) pay more attention to for the simple reason that reading is more central to the normal college curriculum than elementary math skills.

When I worked in admissions, we were always more impressed with a very high verbal score because it was much more indicative of how well a student would do at a school based on a liberal arts curriculum. Perfect 800 math scores were a dime a dozen, but rarely did we see perfect 800 verbal scores.

Here is a summary of how to prep for PSAT and SAT I:

1. Encourage reading from a young age (fifth grade at the latest).
2. Set an example for your children: Be a reader yourself so that they always see that you are reading too.
3. Discuss what you are reading with your children and what they are reading so that they begin to practice their reading comprehension.
4. Check that their school has a vocabulary-building program or take it upon yourself to make them learn ten words a week.
5. By eighth or ninth grade, buy a book of actual SAT I tests from either a bookstore or ETS and pick a quiet weekend so you can have your child take the test and score it.
6. Depending on which section they need the most work on after taking a diagnostic, you may want to hire a tutor or pay for an SAT prep class. If not, you can work from many fine books on how to prepare and work with your children yourself.
7. Stress the importance of the PSAT so that they take this test seriously when it is administered in the tenth grade.

SAT II

These one-hour subject tests were always called "achievement tests" until recently. Though the format has not changed very much, the name has and all the scores have been recentered at a 500 on the 200-to-800 scale. The only other major difference is that now there are many more subject tests available; at last count there were over twenty. Many new subjects have been added, particularly in foreign languages such as Chinese, Japanese, and Hebrew, so students who speak or read and write a second language have an advantage.

Despite what most people think, the SAT II tests are as important, if not more so, than the SAT I because they allow colleges to compare grades from different high schools. If a college is looking at two students, both of whom have A's in English but student A has a 750 on the SAT II subject test and student B has a 580, it is clear that student A is a much better English student and that the A grade is much more accurate at that particular school.

Also, the SAT II tests are very specific in terms of the curriculum they cover: The tests all take one hour and cover a finite amount of material in a certain subject.

If you score low on the biology SAT II, it is evident that you did not learn what you were expected to in high school biology. *A student's aptitude is not as central here as it is in taking the SAT I.* In other words, a student with a very high IQ might score extremely well on the SAT I verbal section because he is a great reader even if he does not study at all. However, no matter how smart that student is, *he cannot get a perfect score on a specific subject test like biology or chemistry unless he learned the material for that subject either on his own or in a class.*

Most colleges require both SAT I and SAT IIs, and the most selective colleges generally require three SAT II tests. Since SAT IIs are offered in over twenty subject areas, the key is to look at the list and start thinking about which are going to be your strong points. Obviously, you don't want to save all three tests until senior year in high school, because there is no way you will do well.

The best strategy is to take the test in June right after the appropriate subject has been covered in school. If your child took biology in ninth grade, he should take the SAT II biology test at the conclusion of the academic year. Because there is an option called "score choice" for SAT IIs, a student can take ten different tests and, once he sees how he scores, he can select or edit which test scores he forwards on to colleges. Therefore, it is okay to take many tests—one or two a year—so that you can accumulate a bank of scores and then send along only your highest to colleges. If you or your child has any uncertainties about this all-important "score choice" option and how to take advantage of it, be sure to seek clarification from either the Educational Testing Service or your guidance counselor.

As parents, one positive step you can take is that when you meet with teachers, ask them what they do to cover the material on the SAT II in their subject area. A good science teacher, for example, will tell you that he not only covers all the material, but he even hands out a practice test or two so students can familiarize themselves with the test before they take it.

If for some reason the school does not do any SAT II preparation, you want to put pressure as concerned parents on the school to have the teachers cover this material. You can form a parents' group, talk to the board of trustees or the PTA—there are many different routes you can take in order to show how strong test results benefit both the students and the high school itself (since the students will get into better colleges).

What a good score consists of is relative to the level of college your children are applying to. At the most general level:

- A score of 750–800 is truly exceptional and a standout at even the most competitive schools.
- 700–750 is excellent.
- 650–700 is sometimes strong enough for the very top colleges if there are other indications that the student shows a deep love of learning.
- 600–650 is just under what the most selective colleges are looking for but very good for the next tier or so down.

- Any score below 600 is solid and strong enough for any college that is not too selective in terms of the percentage of students it can accept.
- A score of 500 would be fine for most state schools or community colleges.

There is not a science to interpreting scores: Colleges look for trends and how these scores measure up to grades. If a student had C's in school but SAT II scores in the high 700s, he would probably be rejected by many top colleges, who would brand him as smart but lazy. Conversely, if a student had all A's in school and low test scores (let's say in the 500s), the college would know that the high school inflated grades and that that student really does not compare with the finest students from across the country.

In short, colleges look for patterns of scores and how these scores either match up or do not match up with grades in high school. In the best of possible cases, a student would show consistency across the board: A terrific spread would be an A student with an SAT I verbal of 740, SAT I math of 700, and SAT II writing score of 730, Math II 710, and Chemistry 760. This combination shows that the student is not only an excellent reader and would do well in courses like history, English, and humanities, but that he is also very solid in math and very good at science, showing strong analytical skills.

It's okay to have one weak area. If math is not your thing, just don't take the SAT II test in math! Play to your strengths—you can take foreign-language tests, science, history, writing, and many others. Why take a subject you are weak in? With over twenty tests to choose from, there is no reason to have one of your three required tests be a subject you hate.

Contrary to what many colleges will tell you outright, these standardized test scores are very important. Without them, colleges have a difficult time comparing students at different schools around the country. In effect, when interpreted correctly, standardized test scores allow admissions officers to compare two things:

1. How do the student's standardized test scores compare to his grades? In other words, does the school grade fairly, does it inflate grades, is it so tough at grading that it needs to use the standardized scores to boost the student?
2. How does the student compare to other students from different states and regions? The benefit of standardized scores is that they allow colleges to compare students from different geographic regions and backgrounds on one set of criteria.

When used well by college admissions officers, standardized tests are extremely revealing and fair. When used poorly (i.e., if the college sets inflexible cutoffs for admissions and does not look at other factors) or in a vacuum (i.e., doesn't compare scores to how the student is doing in the actual subject area), they can be, unfortunately, harmful and unfair.

My general advice is to play with the system. These tests are vital; the more selective the college, the more important it is to do extremely well on these tests. The SAT IIs are relatively easy to prepare for because they are only one-hour tests and *can easily be studied for simply by buying a test review book and going over the material. Start taking the tests in ninth or tenth grade so that you have a bunch of scores to choose from.*

AP and IB Tests

For students who are applying to highly selective colleges, both AP and IB scores are also extremely important—so much so that high scores on these tests can help balance out lower SAT Is or SAT IIs.

The Advanced Placement Program is run by the College Board (ETS, the same people who bring you the SATs) for advanced high school students who take college-level courses in high school. Though some schools allow students to take AP classes as early as tenth grade (generally AP European History), most high schools don't offer AP courses until the student reaches eleventh grade. Please note that in many competitive high schools, there is a rigorous selection process for acceptance into AP courses! High schools may require an A in the previous year's honors-level class, or a certain standardized test score, before they will allow a student to enroll in an AP course—all the more motivation for top students to do well enough in ninth or tenth grade in order to be accepted into these classes.

In May, AP tests are offered in over fifteen different subjects. These tests are meant to be more like college tests, so they are not just multiple choice—almost all the tests have a significant portion of writing or analysis to them. The tests are then sent out to AP graders, so that your individual teacher is not the person who grades them.

These tests are scored on a scale of 1 to 5, with 5 being the highest score. A score of 1 or 2 is considered below par, a 3 is solid, a 4 is very good, and a 5 is excellent. Many colleges award college credit for scores of 4 or 5, so it is definitely to a student's advantage to pay the seventy-five-dollar fee to take the test. As I said earlier, where I went to college, if you had two credits from AP courses you could take an entire trimester off, thereby saving $10,000!

There is also the International Baccalaureate program, which is offered around the world. Rather than offering discrete classes, the IB is more of a "program" in that it is a two-year sequence taken in eleventh and twelfth grades. Usually students who are accepted into the IB program take a pre-IB sequence in ninth and tenth grades (much like honors classes taken before acceptance into AP classes). I find IB more interesting than AP because the curriculum, in my opinion, is more diverse. Rather than offering survey classes, as the AP tends to, IB courses cover more topics in greater depth, mirroring what you do in higher-level college courses. In addition, the IB revises the curriculum every four years to match advances in science, math, and so on, so that it is not as static a curriculum as the AP, which is much slower to change. Finally, the IB is accepted around the world, not just in the United States, so one could apply to Harvard or to the Sorbonne in Paris.

The IB tests are scored on a 1-to-7 scale. A score of 7 is relatively rare, so a 6 is an excellent score, a 5 is very good, even a 4 is considered respectable, with 1–3 being much weaker. A student can take individual IB tests, much like AP tests, but the IB also offers a special diploma for students who follow that whole program, which includes course work, community service, a special course called Theory of Knowledge, and some other facets. It is quite an accomplishment for a high school student to earn the full IB diploma, and it is highly regarded by universities around the world.

Whether a student takes AP or IB courses, the key again is the pattern of scores. A student who takes three AP tests and scores a 5 on all of them shows a very high degree of knowledge in those areas. In many cases, colleges would use an AP score of 5 on the Calculus AB (first year as opposed to BC, which is second year) to wipe out a lower SAT I math or SAT II math score in the 600s, because it is clear that in the more advanced math, this student is quite strong.

Therefore, if a student is applying to highly selective colleges, the best thing he could do would be to score in the 4–5 range on several AP tests or the 6–7 range on IB tests. *Keep in mind that since you apply to college in the fall or early winter, colleges will consider for admission purposes only those test scores taken in the junior year. Therefore, it is to a student's advantage to take AP and IB courses, at least a few, before the senior year.*

Now that we have covered all the major standardized tests, let us turn to how best to utilize summer break.

Chapter 16

What to Do during the Summer

Above all, you want summer to be a time of renewal for your children, a time to learn new skills, practice old ones, to relax, to do activities that might be impossible to squeeze in during the year. However, you do not want to waste summers precisely because we are talking about a ten-week block of time that has tremendous potential for developing your children's physical and mental stamina as well as for developing skills that require longer blocks of time to pick up. I'm not saying that you should force your children into doing academic summer programs against their will, but I am urging parents to encourage their children to make at least part of their summers productive in some tangible way.

Sixth-to-Eighth-Graders

For younger children, you want to mix things up a bit. Between a ten-week summer camp and several activities of shorter duration, I would opt for the latter. At this age, children are just developing proficiency at certain skills, whether they be artistic, athletic, or academic. You want to offer them a palette of activities multicolored enough so that they can try out as many as possible before deciding which ones they would like to concentrate on in the future.

To give you the big picture, the most important thing you want to do is to find out what your children are good at and what they enjoy doing (hopefully the two overlap) in these early years so by the time high school rolls around, they can focus in on one to three different activities at a higher level. I say this because increasingly colleges are not looking for the "well-rounded" student who is a fair athlete, musician, and student. Though in the eighties this was the trend, with the increasing competition for college admission, the most selective colleges look for students who truly excel in one or two areas. In other words, they are looking for *specialists* who reach state and national levels in certain areas rather than *generalists* who do lots of activities, but nothing at a particularly high level.

Let me give you some specific examples. A close family friend's daughter was always a great gymnast. As she got older, she got so good that she started on the Olympic track in the area of rhythmic gymnastics. Her dedication to this one activity meant that she had to give up virtually all normal high school extracurricular activities to fit in the training that eventually led her to the Olympics. Even though she was not a straight-A student (the many practice hours cut in dramatically on her study time) and did no other extracurricular activities besides gymnastics, she got into Cornell University because she had reached such a high level in one area.

Granted, not everyone will reach Olympic level, but it is possible to develop several skills at an early age so that by the time high school rolls around, these skills are very highly developed. Between a three-sport athlete who is a solid player and the All-American lacrosse player, the lacrosse player will always win out in the college arena because he is more valuable to the college.

Likewise, between a mediocre musician who plays in three different school groups and an "All-State" cello player who plays in the National Youth Orchestra, the latter will win because she will be sought after by colleges who are looking to find first-rate musicians for their music groups.

Given this overall view, your job as parents is to be honest with yourself about where your child's talents lie. Don't waste time trying to make a great athlete out of a child who is a great French horn player—you'll just end up frustrating everyone concerned. You want to expose your children to everything: music, athletics, sports like karate or judo, hobbies (model airplanes, jigsaw puzzles, kite flying), reading, computers, and so on, so you can get a feel for what excites them and what they excel in.

Back to how to map out the summers. First of all, no matter where children are during the summer, you always want to stress reading for enjoyment. As I stressed in the last chapter, you will save yourself thousands of dollars in test preparation and much anguish later on if you start working on vocabulary acquisition and reading from an early age. Even if your child goes to camp for all or part of the summer, be sure to have him pack several books he may look forward to reading by the campfire or during quiet time. Make it part of the deal. If you are traveling with your children, set an example yourself by bringing books that you plan on reading and have time set aside for reading during vacations. In this way you lead by example and stress reading at the same time.

Next, work with your children to see what they are interested in. Some will have definite ideas, like "Bobby is doing baseball clinic for two weeks and I want to play with him." In cases like this, try to accommodate their wishes so you can include them in the planning. Try to mix up athletic programs (inexpensive ones usually run through your town's recreation department if you don't want to pay thousands of dollars for fancy clinics and camps) and maybe even some academic activities.

Though many children groan at the thought of more time spent "at school," the number of academic programs available during the summers has skyrocketed in recent years. You don't want to burn out your children; you must be sensitive to their needs and desires. If they absolutely don't want to attend an academic program, perhaps they would prefer working, or breaking up the summer into several different activities.

You need to be a detective. One way to go about it is to read the local newspapers and magazines to see what is being offered in your area during the summer. Start a few months ahead of time so you will have time to think about it. Also, stop by your children's school to see what they have going on in the summer or what flyers they have posted. Check with the town recreation department and any other local groups that run summer activities.

If you are looking for specific areas like whitewater rafting, use the Internet, buy the appropriate magazines (*Outside* magazine would be a great example for all kinds of outdoor activities like hiking, rafting, and kayaking), and visit your local library.

If your child is gifted in math or computer science, find a camp that specializes in these areas. There is no better way to develop these kinds of academic skills in depth than going to a camp with others with like interests. Plus, your children will be surrounded by kids with similar interests, so they are unlikely to be made fun of for being geeks.

In fact, I know scores of children, most of whom are high school age, who love spending their summers in challenging academic programs like those offered by Cornell University, Andover, and Yale, because for once they don't feel like nerds. They realize that there are tons of other children who really enjoy learning. For many children, their discovery of intellectual pursuits takes place in these kinds of summer programs, where there is a real community of learners.

Not all summer activities involve camps or expenditures for sending your children away. For younger children especially, family time is important. Plan a family vacation around an educational theme like wildlife, or national parks or birdwatching. Work on hobbies together; if someone in the family is an avid stamp or coin collector, work with your children at teaching them and working with them to interest them in that field of interest. If you are an amateur astronomer, teach your children. Here are some hobbies and activities that are great to learn at a young age and to continue on in more depth as children grow older:

1. Coin or stamp collecting
2. Model cars or trains
3. Proficiency at sports
4. Any kind of martial art like judo or karate
5. Backyard astronomy
6. Music collecting and education
7. Home repair or projects that involve handiwork
8. Computer programming
9. Writing projects (books, novels)
10. Jigsaw puzzles
11. Hunting
12. Archery
13. Riflery or sports like trap and skeet
14. Mountain or road biking
15. Collecting baseball or any kind of sports cards
16. Sewing or making your own clothes

As you can see, there are multitudes of areas to get involved in. If you are lacking in creative ideas, visit a hobby shop. Just talking to those who work there will spark many ideas. Again, visit a library and look through books about hobbies and pastimes. Childhood, especially the years in sixth to eighth grade, is a time to really enjoy these kinds of activities. They should be fun for your children and fun for you.

Ninth Grade through Eleventh Grade

By the time your children reach high school age, you want to help them narrow down their interests and become very good in a few areas. If they like music, focus on that area by providing lessons, mandating practice time, and encouraging them to join several in-school or out-of-school music groups. If athletics is their strength, focus on this area by supporting their practices and games and by finding competitive summer leagues. If they like writing, volunteer to help them proofread and edit, find organizations like the school literary magazine or newspaper that require and refine good writing skills.

Remember that not all their pursuits have to be through school. If their interest lies in a field like martial arts or dance, it's possible that these are all offered by local venues other than schools. That's okay because colleges don't really distinguish between in-school and out-of-school activities as long as a student shows that he has reached a high level of skill.

In a nutshell, your job as parents is to foster and develop your children's interests during summers so that they will gain self-esteem and develop their own natural talents. You want to challenge them without burning them out. If they are not having fun, something is wrong. There's nothing wrong with some unscheduled time during the summers, but you want to provide enough structure so that they will have the building blocks they will need later on for pursuing their areas of interest.

Chapter 17

Extracurricular Activities

In the last chapter we spent time talking about how best to utilize summers either to find new interests or to practice and develop old ones. Much of what is true for summer activities is true for extracurricular activities, too. As we discussed, colleges are looking for students with a few specific talents, hobbies, and passions rather than those who have many interests but few real talents.

Thus, the same theory holds for sixth-to-eighth-graders as in the last chapter: At this age, encourage your children to sign up for a variety of activities so they can experiment and find out what they are talented in. If your children are athletic, by all means let them play a sport each season. If they are musical, let them try out jazz band, choir, and symphony, to find out what they enjoy the most. If they become interested in an out-of-school activity like judo or karate, let them pursue that for a while to see if they find it interesting.

Your job as parents is to foster and encourage your children's interests. If they are reluctant to try anything, your job as parents is to stress that it takes time to develop any talent and no one just starts an activity and is immediately great at it.

This last lesson is important enough to dwell on for a moment. Some children are fast learners, and some are slow learners. It is frustrating for a slow learner to go out on the soccer field with friends and realize that it is taking him longer to pick up basic skills than some of his teammates. When you see your child's frustration level rising to such an extent that he shies away from trying anything new, you need to step in and gently encourage him. Just because it may take longer to learn a certain skill does not mean that the slow learner will not ultimately be better at it than the quick learner.

Let the middle school years be a period when your children are involved in many different activities with an eye toward focusing on fewer once it is time to enter high school.

By the time your children reach high school age, you will know where at least some of their talents lie. It is rare to find a tenth-grader who suddenly tries playing soccer and rises to national level. Most skills take years to develop to the point where one reaches a very high level, so take an honest look at your children and encourage them to pursue their most important passions.

Remember, colleges do not distinguish between in-school and out-of-school activities, so it is perfectly acceptable to take dance lessons five days a week at a local college or to go to judo class as long as it is clear to the college that the activity requires many hours a week. Any activity that shows consistent follow-through for several years is meaningful. When colleges ask students to list their activities, they ask how many hours a week the activity takes up. What they are not impressed by are lists of many unconnected activities that require only 1 to 2 hours a week. They much prefer to see a select number with high weekly hours because the odds are that this kind of devotion will lead to a high level of proficiency.

Don't be afraid to be different! Just because all of your children's classmates are athletic does not mean that they can't follow their own interests in something totally different. Remember, colleges are looking for unusual talents because it helps set apart those students who are truly interesting and different. They will receive tons of applications from athletes who are proficient in two or three sports, but they don't get too many students who started their own small business by using their talent in computer programming to help local stores set up computer systems.

What if Extras Are Taking Away from Academic Time?

Of course there needs to be a balance between academics and extras, but you as parents have to be mindful of the tension that develops when extras start cutting into academic time. Rather than asking your children to immediately cut back on their extras, remind them that some of the most competitive students in the country do balance an extraordinary combination of academic rigor (all honors and AP or IB classes) with a heavy load of extracurricular activities. In fact, the typical high achiever manages to graduate in the top of his high school class while being captain of three sports teams, class president, and an all-state musician.

Thus, you don't want to panic your children when they have to pull an all-nighter to write a paper; rather, you want to help them go back to the drawing board for time management so they can see how to find free hours during the week without dropping extra activities right away. Help your children by reading this list of tips for using time well.

Where to Find Time When There Seems to Be None

1. Make good use of any free periods in school—if you have a study hall or a long lunch period, try to get a start on your homework during this time. However, it is *not* a good idea to use a boring teacher's class time to do the coming night's homework! First, you'll miss what the teacher is teaching that day. Second, the teacher will notice your inat-

tention and will mark you down accordingly for lower grades in class participation.

2. If you take any kind of public transportation to get to school, use that time to go over notes, read, or study.

3. Be organized: Don't waste precious time sitting around thinking about what you need to do—have it all mapped out as we discussed in earlier chapters.

4. Use the weekends to catch up and get ahead for the week. If you know you'll be expected to read a good amount of a novel by the following Friday, get a jump on it on Sunday.

5. Do your English and history reading on the weekend, when you have longer chunks of time. It is much more efficient to read a novel in one long block of time broken up with small breaks and then reread it during the week than to try to keep up with long reading assignments on a nightly basis.

6. If you find yourself falling behind, use vacation time to catch up and then get ahead by staying way ahead in reading or paper-writing. Think of vacations as a time to work leisurely on schoolwork rather than taking a full week off and then having to play catch-up once you get back.

7. If you get overwhelmed during the week, it is okay every once in a while to skip all your extracurriculars. I know it is difficult in sports, but on a day when you have practice with no game in the near future, tell your coach what is going on and see if you can get a day off. Sometimes just one long day without extras can help you catch up.

8. If you get stuck on homework problems during the week, call a friend or study partner in the same class and see if you can work together on solving them. It is a good idea to study with a friend anyway, particularly one who might be good in a subject like physics that you might be weak in.

In short, think long and hard before you quit a team or drop an extracurricular activity in the middle of the year. Colleges will judge you on your ability to follow through with your interests and do not like to see students bail out at the first sign of hardship.

Chapter 18

Get a Job!

One of the best things you can do for your children is not to spoil them and to teach them that they cannot have everything they want. On the one hand, we want to help our children and to give them what they need for success. What we need to keep in mind, though, is that what we give our children does not have to be material in nature—in fact, the most valuable things we can give our children are intangibles like support, love, care, time, and understanding.

One way to teach your children responsibility is to make them responsible for helping out with household chores like doing dishes, taking out the garbage, cooking, and helping with child care. The other way to teach them responsibility is to encourage them to get a job so they see how hard it is to earn the money they are so keen on spending.

Fiscal responsibility cannot be taught in the abstract: If your child decides he needs a $200 Walkman and gets it just by asking, he really has no concept of what that money represents. But if he were, for example, working at Burger King on weekends and making five dollars an hour, he could equate that $200 to an actual effort: over forty hours of hard work.

Plus, if a child makes some income on his own, it affords a great opportunity to teach him about what to do with money besides spending it. Show your children how to invest money in the stock market and in mutual funds, how to track money and keep track of interest. Show them how interest compounds and that $1,000 invested when they are fifteen years old could turn into hundreds of thousands by the time they retire. Think of all the lifelong skills you can pass along to your children, even when they are only in middle school.

Looking at the big picture, there are many advantages to having a paid job besides the very valuable ones I just mentioned. Many colleges are biased against students who have had everything in life handed to them. After all, if you were looking at two students with very similar academic records but one went to fancy private schools all his life and had everything paid for from music lessons to horseback riding, whereas the other one grew up in an inner-city neighborhood and had to pay for everything himself, the less advantaged student will always win out. Holding down a job over a period of time is the best way to offset a privileged background.

A college can't hold it against a student if his parents are wealthy and he goes to an excellent school, but it can hold him up to very high expectations. For example, if you are an admissions officer and you can see that the child has taken drum lessons for fifteen years but is still not a very good drummer, it is easy to say something like "Even all that money can't buy talent."

That is why I always encourage students I work with to get a job, even if it's a manual-labor, grunt-work type of job, because this is the best way to show that a student can feel for others who are not part of his social class. Of course, another smart path to pursue is to help your children find a job that backs up their academic interests. A student who loves science and research can often find a job working in a local college laboratory doing experimental work, just as a student interested in medicine can volunteer to work in a hospital. Many volunteer jobs can turn into paid jobs once a student gains experience.

Many times high schools run vocational programs or are affiliated with local businesses, so students of all backgrounds can take advantage of job opportunities offered through the high school. As a parent, you can do some of the research involved in finding out what types of jobs are available. Don't be afraid to use connections if your neighbors or friends work in areas that might be of interest to your children.

If you can start your children on the job path at the end of middle school, even if it's only a few hours a week, you are giving them a chance to establish a connection with an employer. It's a nice touch to get a letter of recommendation from an employer saying that your child was a long-term asset to his business.

While it's always a good thing to do community service, it is much less common for students to hold a steady job. Plus, some schools require community service (in fact, many more than you might imagine do), so colleges tend not to be very impressed with community service unless it's truly extraordinary because it's so common, not to mention required in many schools.

One final fact about jobs: Many parents are against the idea because they feel that working will take away time from homework. While at first this seems like a valid concern, keep in mind that students who work, just like athletes who compete in games all week, learn how to balance time and tend not to waste it. In other words, students with major time commitments learn to manage their time more effectively.

The typical student who gets home from school every day at four o'clock because he has no extra activities statistically does no better academically than the busy student who gets home much later. In fact, educational studies have shown that students who participate in many different extras have a higher success rate academically than those who do very little. The student who gets home early tends to waste a lot of time by watching TV, hanging out with friends, or just stretching homework time out over many hours instead of prioritizing and trying to complete work in a timely manner.

Start with a job with a reasonable weekly time requirement (at first, let's say just some shifts on weekends) and let it expand if the interest is there. The benefits of holding down a regular job in high school extend well beyond just showing responsibility: Working at a job will help your children learn the value of a dollar, become more independent, establish a sense of pride, learn relevant job skills, and force them to manage their time better, not to mention bucking any class stereotypes having to do with coming from an affluent background.

Chapter 19

Eye on the Prize: Looking Ahead to College

Whether your children aspire to attend the most elite universities in the country or the local community college, the decision about where to attend college will be one of the most important decisions they make in their lifetime.

Clearly, not every American child will go on to college. There are those who, for specific reasons, are actually better off going directly into a trade or profession from high school. However, for the majority of those students who do not go on to earn a college degree, there is the chance that they are seriously limiting their future in terms of job prospects, income level, and quality of life. Where your children go to college will influence their friends for the next twenty years, the development of their intellect, perhaps the part of the country they will make connections and live in, the professional career they may choose, and many other aspects of their future lives.

The problem is that for middle school-age children, the prospect of college seems so distant that many cannot attach any immediacy to it. Also, a parent does not want to instill in a child panicky anxiety about the far-off future. For a typical fourteen-year-old, being invited to Joey's birthday party next weekend is much more important than doing well in school so eventually he can select a first-choice college.

However, there are steps you as a parent can take to ensure that your children will at least be able to aim high and see the future, no matter how distant it may seem at first.

If your child has any kind of athletic interest, either as a spectator or a participant, find a local college or take a trip to the nearest big university and attend some sporting events. For many students, sports will be the easiest entry point or at least a point of interest. I've seen fifth-graders who are already sure they want to attend a certain university just because the school has a strong sports team that they follow. It's okay to have the preliminary interest be non-academic in nature because the academic piece will come much later in the game anyway. Besides, you can always add facts like, "Did you know that to make the football team at School X you have to have a 3.0 GPA?"

What children see when they attend sporting events at the college level is the tremendous amount of school spirit exhibited by both the players and the fans, whether it be participating in the game with enthusiasm, dressing up as the mascot, painting themselves the school colors, or cheering vociferously for their team.

If you have any friends or family who have a son or daughter who is interested in serving as a buddy for your child, try to set up either an E-mail exchange or a personal meeting during college breaks so that they can get together. Having an older role model who can discuss the positive aspects of college is another way to influence and motivate young children.

Finally, when your children are slightly older (eighth or ninth grade), incorporate some informal college visits during family vacations. While it is not appropriate to drag your children to twelve colleges over their spring break, combining a Thanksgiving holiday in Vermont with a visit to Middlebury College and touring the campus will give your children an idea of how impressive many college campuses are. Try to pick a campus with a very "campusy" feeling such as Cornell; choose any college or university major enough to have a sizable physical plant.

You want your child to be dazzled by the many impressive features of a well-endowed campus: the library, the natatorium (a building with swimming pools), the domed astronomy observatory, the campus center for dramatic arts, the science buildings with their state-of-the-art laboratories, the music building with concert halls and practice rooms.

Even children who think of their own middle schools or high schools as prison-like (and therefore associate all colleges with a similar atmosphere) are often surprised to find out how much more pleasant a college campus can be than their own school's.

If you take steps like these toward introducing your children to college in subtle ways, you may be able to inspire them early on to do their best in middle school and high school so they will have a good chance of attending their first-choice college.

How to Keep Current on the Changes in College Admissions

While your children do not need to be worrying about things like changing college admission requirements and financial aid, it is important that you as parents keep current.

For example, if you hadn't been looking or following college admissions for a while, you might not even know about the major changes I mentioned earlier in scoring the SAT I and SAT II tests. How can you as parents keep current?

One way is to read a major newspaper like the *New York Times* or the *Wall Street Journal* on a regular basis. Both major newspapers and magazines like *Time, Newsweek,* and *U.S. News & World Report* have regular features on higher education in which they report on important changes. All the recent changes in financial aid, for example, were reported on by all the above publications.

Use the Internet! There are many great Web sites that help with general college information. Plus every major college or university has its own Web site, which goes over everything from how many books there are in the library to what the admission standard is. The following are some helpful general college Internet sites:

College Board Search: www.collegeboard.org
Peterson's Undergraduate Program Search:
   www.petersons.com/ugrad/search
College Edge: www.collegeedge.com
FishNet—The College Guide: www.jayi.com
College Net: www.collegenet.com
College View: www.collegeview.com
The Universal Black Pages: www.ubp.com
Hillel: www.hillel.org
Princeton Review: www.princetonreview.com

Also, use any major search engine (www.yahoo.com or www.dogpile.com) and search under "higher education" to find links to all the nation's colleges and universities.

Even if your children are only in middle school, read the local paper and show up at public events that pertain to colleges. Many high schools invite the major-college representatives to their campuses to talk about college admission, and you don't have to have a child in high school to show up! Don't drag your children to them, but go to as many of these events as you can so you can stay abreast of all the major changes. You can then report on relevant information as it comes up. For example, if your child has mentioned that he is interested in attending a selective college but hates doing homework, you can mention that you just went to a presentation by the Amherst representative and found out that 45 percent of the incoming class graduated either number one or number two in their high schools.

Obviously, you want to present these findings in a constructive way so that your children can feel they have a chance of improving. There is no need to discourage them by saying something to the effect of "Well, don't bother because Amherst only accepts smart kids." In general, try to state things in the positive rather than the negative. Instead of saying "If you don't get all A's, you'll never get into a top college," try "Do your best to get as many A's as possible so you can take a shot at a top college."

Your major concern should be to gather facts a little bit at a time between roughly seventh grade and eleventh grade so that when it comes time to apply to college, you are not caught off guard. Informed parents are of much greater service to their children than uninterested parents who put all the burden on their children to find out about college choices.

Even the brightest children don't have time to devote to this kind of exhaustive college research, because if they spend all their spare time hunting down information, how can they devote the time to their studies that will help them get into a selective school in the first place?

Think of yourself as a filter: You will receive and hunt down tons of information on college admissions over a period of several years, but you will distill and highlight only the points that are relevant to your children. Your job will be greatly simplified anyway, because by the time your children take the preliminary SAT National Merit Qualifying Test (the PSAT-NMQT), they will be automatically put on a good number of college mailing lists. The higher their scores, the more selective the colleges that send material and catalogs to your home.

Once you have helped your children to the point where they are ready to apply to college, it might be time to pick up for them a copy of *A Is for Admission,* which treats the subject exhaustively. Although it is geared toward those applying to highly selective colleges, the majority of information (such as filling out the application and taking various standardized tests) applies to almost all colleges. Good luck!

Appendix A

Web Sites for Help with Homework

1. Education Resources Homework Helper
   www.startribune.com/education/homework.shtml   K–12

2. Homework Central—tons of information for all ages
   www.homeworkcentral.com   K–12

3. Jumpsite to many different homework resources
   www.zen.org/-brendan/kids-homework.html   K–12
   Excellent!

4. Homework Hotline On-line Schoolhouse
   www.wvptv.wvnet.edu/homework/hhmain.htm   K–12

5. Great Homework Help site—has tons of information on almost every school subject
   www.jiskha.com   K–12

6. Very Helpful Math Web Site—just enter in the problem and get step-by-step instructions on how to solve it
   www.webmath.com Excellent!   K–12

7. Test-taking Strategies and Tips
   www.unb.ca/web/courses/fields/module/textbook/chlpt5d.html
   4–12

8. Learning to Learn—diagnose your own weaknesses and learn how to improve them
   www.snow.utoronto.ca/Learn2/introll.html   4–12

9. Test Taking Skills for Essay Exams
   www.osb.org/advising/help/testskil.html   4–12

10. Test Taking Skills—tips on improving test taking skills
    www.austin.cc.tx.us/lrs/testtake.htm   4–12

11. Study Skills—jumpsite to study tips on the Internet
    www.ouacinfo.ouac.on.ca/osca/study-tips.htm   4–12
    Excellent!

12. Suggestions for Test Taking and Studying
www.web.couns.msu.edu/self-help/testaking.htm   4–12

Good General Search Engines:
www.dogpile.com gives you the results of several major search engines without having to run many different searches.
www.alltheweb.com is one of the best multi-engine searches available.

Appendix B

School Supplies

The Basics

The first essential component of being organized is having the right school supplies for the job. After all, even if you are the most organized carpenter in the world, you still can't work on a house unless you have the proper tools. The most basic supplies are pens and pencils, plus a portable pencil sharpener and a little plastic bag that clips into a notebook or binder so that the student is never without writing utensils. As far as pencils are concerned, I recommend a number 2 or number 1 lead pencil rather than a number 3 because the lead is softer and writes darker so that you don't have to push down on it as hard. Since pencils are quite inexpensive, be sure to include at least five in your child's plastic pouch, along with a small sharpener.

Most parents overlook the importance of pen quality, but given the fact that we as a country do such a poor job teaching penmanship, most of our children grow up with handwriting that is barely legible. Although it is true that many of us grow up to do most of our writing on computers, all students generally will need to write neatly by hand on college applications, on AP exams, on surprise tests and quizzes in high school, and during most classes to take notes. In choosing a pen for young students, I would pick a very smooth-writing ballpoint pen and then buy two with black ink and two with blue ink. I would not buy pens with erasable ink because they do not write as smoothly and the ink looks messy when erased. I would also not get roller-ball pens because young children tend to smear the ink before it dries.

My favorite inexpensive pen (in the three-to-four-dollar range) is the Paper Mate Dynagrip RT 50 ballpoint pen with the rubber pad around the barrel. It writes extremely well and is very comfortable to hold. It costs a little bit more than a generic cheap pen, but the few extra dollars are dollars well spent.

If you want to splurge on one nice pen (assuming your child will put it back in the plastic pouch when done and will not lose it!), buy one of the Sensa brand pens, which are the most comfortable to write with and in fact have won many design awards for their perfect ergonomic design (and they look cool, too). They have a soft gel around the barrel that actually molds to your child's grip—the modern-day equivalent of what we used to call "grippers" that slid over your pencil. Though it seems extravagant to spend $25 to $45 on a pen like this, think of all the holiday money that is wasted on more expensive items like video games and gadgets that have little practical purpose.

Now that your child has this plastic pouch all filled with writing utensils, he needs a good notebook to clip the pouch into and to keep track of all his classes. While there are many cheap three-ring binders, I have found that it's worth the money to buy a good one, since children will probably use the same notebook all year. Since those that have perfectly round rings tend to crunch the paper at the end and the front, I find that the best ones are those that have rings that rise up at a sharp angle and then slope gently downward to the right in a straight line (called "D ring").

As you can imagine, this kind of system fans the paper out so that the paper at the end stays spread out to the right instead of getting sucked back under and ripped out. Also, check out the rings: Are they sturdy, or are they already having trouble opening and closing without snagging if you play with them a little? If you really want to avoid the problem of paper falling out and ripping at the holes, invest in the great paper made by Aigner Index, Inc. Their address and phone number is: 218 MacArthur Avenue, New Windsor, NY 12553, 1-800-242-3919. Their Web site is holdex@frontier.net. Their paper has a clear plastic band down the left side of the paper that reinforces the holes. The paper itself is quite heavyweight, very smooth, and comes lined, college-ruled, and unlined.

Finally, you will want a binder that is as industrial as possible—no paper, no light material. The best ones usually have a rubber-type coating. Remember, your child is going to be shoving this notebook in and out of his bookbag thousands of times before the year is out, so you want to invest in the sturdiest possible notebook. Be sure to check with your children's teachers before buying notebooks, because often they will be extremely picky about what they require.

Paper

For young students (sixth-to-eighth-graders) I recommend wide-ruled paper for the notebook because it is easier to write on and it's better that they write a little bigger until their handwriting improves. Older students may prefer college-ruled (more narrow-lined) paper, particularly if they have small but neat handwriting. Be sure to have your child write his name in indelible ink in at least two different places in the notebook in case it gets lost during the year (a very distinct possibility), and clip his name in the plastic pouch right in the front.

The Homework Notebook

I think your best bet is to go with a medium-sized homework notebook, around five inches by eight inches. If your child uses a minipad, it will probably get lost and, in addition, it is very difficult to keep a chart of day-to-day assignments. If your child uses a full-sized notebook, it will be much like the three-ring binder in that he will be unlikely to pull it out to write down last-minute assignments. Once again, make sure to ask your child to write his name at least two or three times on the notebook.

The Backpack or Schoolbag

Now that we have most of our supplies (and there will be some extra supplies I haven't mentioned: for the math teacher who wants a one-subject spiral notebook and/or a compass, ruler, or small calculator, for example), we turn to helping your child learn how to organize the backpack. As I emphasized in picking a binder, the backpack is an item that will suffer tremendous abuse during the year, so I recommend that you invest a few extra dollars up front if at all possible to buy one that is very sturdy (definitely not an all-nylon one because they fray very quickly and rip) and made of an industrial-strength canvas or other strong material.

You'll want the knapsack to have at a minimum an inside compartment for notebooks and textbooks and an outside compartment for smaller items like extra pens and pencils and the homework notebook. It should also have comfortable and well-padded shoulder straps so that even a small child can tighten up the straps and carry a heavy bag without injuring his back. It is an excellent idea to have your child try the bag on, or at least to make sure that the straps are adjustable enough that the child will be able to tighten them enough to pull the load right against his back.

You need to impress upon your child the importance of taking a minute at the end of the school day to look at the homework assignments in order to figure out which books he will need to bring home.

Appendix C

Suggested Middle School Reading List

This is only a suggested list. If your child is an advanced reader, feel free to jump up a grade. Conversely, if he is a weak reader, pick from a list a grade level or two below the grade he is now in.

Fifth and Sixth Grade (from ALA Best Books List)

Belle Prater's Boy	Ruth White
Crash	Jerry Spinella
Gideon's People	Carolyn Meyer
Sabriel	Garth Nix
Slam!	Walter Dean Myers
The Thief	Megan Whalen Turner
Drummers of Jericho	Carolyn Meyer
Like Sisters on the Home Front	Rita Williams-Garcia
Thwonk	Joan Bauer
The Watsons Go to Birmingham, 1963	Christopher Paul Curtis
We Are the Witnesses	Jacob Boas
Companions of the Night	Vivian Vande Velde
The King's Shadow	Elizabeth Alder
Little Girls in Pretty Boxes	Joan Ryan
One Bird	Kyoko Mori
The Only Alien on the Planet	Kristen D. Randle
Under the Mermaid Angel	Martha Moore

Survival and Adventure Novels

Alas, Babylon	Pat Frank
The Cay	Theodore Taylor
The Girl Who Owned a City	O. T. Nelson
Snow Bound: A Story of Raw Survival	Harry Mazer

Wolf-Woman	Sheryl Jordan
The River	Gary Paulsen
A Deadly Promise	Joan Lowery Nixon
Adventure on the Graveyard of the Wrecks	Ola Cossi
The Remarkable Journey of Prince Jen	Lloyd Alexander
Hatchet	Gary Paulsen
Lost in the Devil's Desert	Gloria Skorzynski
Year of Impossible Goodbyes	Sook Nyul Choi
Adrift: Seventy-Six Days Lost at Sea	Steve Callahan
The Girl in the Box	Ovida Sebestyen

Revolutionary War

April Morning	Howard Fast
Johnny Tremaine	Esther Forbes
My Brother Sam Is Dead	James Lincoln Collier
Sarah Bishop	Scott O'Dell

Civil War

Across Five Aprils	Irene Hunt
The Boys' War	Jim Murphy
Rifles for Watie	Harold Keith

World War II

Summer of My German Soldier	Betty Green
The Bomb	Theodore Taylor
The Kingdom by the Sea	Robert Westall
Friedrich	Hans P. Richter
The Boys from St. Petri	Bjarne Reuter
Farewell to Manzanar	Jeanne Houston

Newbury Honor Books

Bridge to Terabithia	Katherine Peterson
Dicey's Song	Cynthia Voigt
The Giver	Lois Lowry
The High King	Lloyd Alexander

Roll of Thunder, Hear My Cry	Mildred Taylor
The Slave Dancer	Paula Fox
Walk Two Moons	Sharon Creech
A Wrinkle in Time	Madeleine L'Engle
The Moves Make the Man	Bruce Brooks
Old Yeller	Fred Gipson
Shabanu: Daughter of the Wind	Suzanne Fisher Staples
The Great Fire	Jim Murphy
Dragon's Gate	Laurence Yep
Nothing but the Truth	Avi
Yolanda's Genius	Carol Fenner

For Girls Especially

The Midwife's Apprentice	Karen Cushman
I Am an Artichoke	Lucy Frank
Circles	Marilyn Sachs
Dusty Branigan	Avi
Friends First	Christine McDonnell

For Boys Especially

Jumping the Nail	Eve Bunty
Mariposa Blues	Ron Koertge
Slake's Limbo	Felice Holman
The Circlemaker	Maxine Rose Schur
The Rebounder	Thomas Dygard

Seventh and Eighth Grade

Shane	Jack Schaefer
The Hobbit	J. R. R. Tolkein
In Country	Bobbie Ann Mason
The Education of Little Tree	Forrest Carter
The Bean Trees	Barbara Kingsolver
A Raisin in the Sun	Lorraine Hansberry
Black Boy	Richard Wright
In Our Time	Ernest Hemingway

Let Us Now Praise Famous Men	James Agee
The Martian Chronicles	Ray Bradbury
The House on Mango Street	Sandra Cisneros
David Copperfield	Charles Dickens
The Water Is Wide	Pat Conroy
When Legends Die	Hal Borland
A Wrinkle in Time	Madeleine L'Engle
Island of the Blue Dolphins	Scott O'Dell
Go Ask Alice	Anonymous
That Was Then, This Is Now	S. E. Hinton
The Witch of Blackbird Pond	Elizabeth Speare
The Chocolate War	Robert Cormier
A Summer to Die	Lois Lowry
A Door into Summer	Robert Heinlein
A Walk in Wolf Wood	Mary Stewart
A Gift of Magic	Lois Duncan
Acorn People	Ron Jones
Am I Blue	Marion Dane Bauer
Athletic Shorts	Chris Crutcher
Baby	Patricia Maclachlan
Canyons	Gary Paulsen
Chronicles of Narnia	C. S. Lewis
Citizen of the Galaxy	Robert Heinlein
Coming out of Silence	Marion Dane Bauer

Going into Ninth Grade/Advanced

When the Legends Die	Hal Borland
Jane Eyre	Charlotte Brontë
The Ox-Box Incident	Walter Van Tilburg Clark
Sleeping Arrangements	Laura Cunningham
Black Like Me	John Howard Griffen
Rebecca	Daphne du Maurier
Hiroshima	John Hersey
The Boys of Summer	Roger Kahn

Annie John	Jamaica Kincaid
One Fat Summer	Robert Lipsyte
The Boys from Brazil	Ira Levin
A Night to Remember	Walter Lord
Lovey: A Very Special Child	Mary MacCracken
The Forty-third War	Louise Moeri
Anne of Green Gables	Lucy Maud Montgomery
The Learning Tree	Gordon Parks
The Chosen	Chaim Potok
Where the Red Fern Grows	Wilson Rawls
Treasure Island	Robert Louis Stevenson
A Tree Grows in Brooklyn	Betty Smith
Ladder of Years	Anne Tyler
The Lord of the Rings (Trilogy)	J. R. R. Tolkein
The Once and Future King	T. H. White
The City Boy	Herman Wouk
Fantastic Voyage	Isaac Asimov
Watership Down	Richard Adams
The Hitchhiker's Guide to the Galaxy	Douglas Adams
Cold, Sassy Tree	Olive Ann Burns
In Cold Blood	Truman Capote
The Great Train Robbery	Michael Crichton
Having Our Say	Elizabeth Delaney
Eva	Peter Dickinson
The Bride Price	Buchi Emecheta
Father Melancholy's Daughter	Gail Godwin
Death Be Not Proud	John Gunther
Summer of '49	David Halberstam
All Creatures Great and Small	James Herriot
Girl, Interrupted	Susanna Kaysen
Pigs in Heaven	Barbara Kingsolver
Peace Breaks Out	John Knowles
Out of the Silent Planet	C. S. Lewis
My Name Is Asher Lev	Chaim Potok
The Chosen	Chaim Potok

Iron and Silk	Mark Salzman
A Daughter of Time	Josephine Tey
The Accidental Tourist	Anne Tyler
Jubilee	Margaret Walker
Soldiers in Hiding	Richard Wiley

Advanced Ninth Grade and Up

American Classics

Death Comes for the Archbishop	Willa Cather
Absalom Absalom	William Faulkner
As I Lay Dying	William Faulkner
The Sound and the Fury	William Faulkner
The Great Gatsby	F. Scott Fitzgerald
The House of the Seven Gables	Nathaniel Hawthorne
Their Eyes Were Watching God	Zora Neale Hurston
The Ambassadors	Henry James
Uncle Tom's Cabin	Harriet Beecher Stowe
Huckleberry Finn	Mark Twain
Native Son	Richard Wright

Some of My Favorites

The Unconsoled	Kazuo Ishiguro
The Remains of the Day	Kazuo Ishiguro
Artist of the Floating World	Kazuo Ishiguro
The Mambo Kings Play Songs of Love	Oscar Hijuelos
This Boy's Life	Tobias Wolff
A Confederacy of Dunces	John Kennedy Toole
Ellen Foster	Kaye Gibbons
Mrs. Caliban	Rachel Ingalls
A Simple Plan	Scott Smith
The Stranger	Albert Camus
The Plague	Albert Camus
Madame Bovary	Gustave Flaubert

Any book by T. Coraghessan Boyle

Corelli's Mandolin	Louis De Bernieres
The Painted Bird	Jerzy Kosinski
Woman Warrior	Maxine Kingston
Cane	Jean Toomer
Saint Maybe	Anne Tyler
The Color Purple	Alice Walker
Lempriere's Dictionary	Lawrence Norfolk
All Quiet on the Western Front	Erich Remarque
The Three Musketeers	Alexandre Dumas
All the King's Men	Robert Penn Warren
Last of the Mohicans	James Fenimore Cooper
Perfume	Patrick Suskind
Paris Trout	Pete Dexter
The Moonstone	Wilkie Collins
Woman in White	Wilkie Collins
Dreaming in Cuban	Cristina Garcia
Like Water for Chocolate	Laura Esquivel
Bones of the Moon	Jonathan Carroll
Voice of Our Shadow	Jonathan Carroll
Outside the Dog Museum	Jonathan Carroll
After Silence	Jonathan Carroll
The Elephant Vanishes	Haruki Murakami
A Wild Sheep Chase	Haruki Murakami
Hard Boiled Wonderland and The End of the World	Haruki Murakami
Dance, Dance, Dance	Haruki Murakami
The Dork of Cork	Chet Raymo
Pale Fire	Vladimir Nabokov
Speak, Memory	Vladimir Nabokov
The Drowned and the Saved	Primo Levi
Martin Dressler	Steven Millhauser
Memoirs of a Geisha	Arthur Golden
Wild Swans: Three Daughters of China	Jung Chang
The Solitaire Mystery	Jostein Gaarder

British Classics

Sense and Sensibility	Jane Austen
Pride and Prejudice	Jane Austen
Persuasion	Jane Austen
Wuthering Heights	Charlotte Brontë
Great Expectations	Charles Dickens
Oliver Twist	Charles Dickens
A Tale of Two Cities	Charles Dickens
Tess of the D'Urbervilles	Thomas Hardy
To the Lighthouse	Virginia Woolf

Great Novellas

The Awakening	Kate Chopin
Daisy Miller	Henry James
The Turn of the Screw	Henry James
Death in Venice	Thomas Mann
The Secret Sharer	Joseph Conrad
Ethan Frome	Edith Wharton
The Picture of Dorian Gray	Oscar Wilde

Prize Winners

Possession	A. S. Byatt
The Adventures of Augie March	Saul Bellow
The Beginning and the End	Naguib Mahfouz
The Butcher Boy	Patrick McCabe
All the Pretty Horses	Cormac McCarthy
House Made of Dawn	Scott Momaday
Song of Solomon	Toni Morrison
Enemies: A Love Story	Isaac Bashevis Singer

Appendix D

Math Guidelines

Obviously, there is no "national" math curriculum in our country. Even so, there are some basic concepts that are so fundamental that I feel comfortable saying that students should have covered them by certain times. Below you will find a rough guideline to major milestones of middle school math achievement. They are not meant to represent any one school, but rather any middle school that maintains a solid math program.

Fifth Grade

Students should have *mastered:*

- Computation (addition, subtraction, multiplication, and division) of whole numbers
- Computation—decimals
- Computation—proper fractions
- Expressing fractions in simplest form
- Rounding numbers
- Reading, writing, and understanding of place value—whole numbers and decimals
- Recognizing prime and composite numbers
- Measurement in the standard system
- Telling time
- Changing between units of time
- Identifying polygons by the number of sides
- Finding simple perimeters
- Measuring and drawing angles using a protractor
- Critical thinking skills: solving word problems involving all of the above concepts

Students should be introduced to:

- Computation—mixed numbers
- Prime factorization
- Greatest Common Factor (GCF), Least Common Multiple (LCM)
- Statistics—mean, median, mode
- Measurement in the metric system
- Integers
- Area of geometric figures
- Circumference and area of circles
- Percents
- Graph ordered pairs on the coordinate plane

Sixth Grade

Mastery:

- Computation of whole numbers, decimals, fractions, mixed numbers
- Number theory: prime factorization, GCF, LCM, rules of divisibility
- Statistics: mean, median, mode
- Measurement in the metric system
- Perimeter and area of geometric figures
- Critical thinking skills: solving word problems involving all of the above concepts

Introduction:

- Integers, placing them in order on the number line
- Simple algebraic equations and the solutions
- Graphs: circle, bar, line, and when to use them appropriately
- Percents: definitions, using them in problems

Differences usually occur at this point. If a child takes seventh-grade math the following should occur: mastery of all of the sixth-grade concepts at a slightly higher level. If a child goes into pre-algebra at this point, it is expected that those concepts have already been mastered.

By the End of Pre-Algebra

The following is expected:

- Computation of integers and rational numbers
- Solving equations of degree 1, with the variable on both sides of the equation
- Understanding and solving simple inequalities
- Solutions of geometry problems using algebra (equations)
- Ratio, proportions, and rate
- Percents: finding the percent of a number, finding the base when the percent is known, finding the percent when the percent and base are known
- Problem-solving using all of these concepts

Annotated Bibliography

ADD Warehouse: 1-800-233-9273 A great source of teaching materials and reading materials for students with attention deficit disorder.

Carter, William Lee. *The Angry Teenager: Why Teens Get So Angry, and How Parents Can Help Them Grow Through It*. Nashville, TN: Tommy Nelson, 1995. Written from the perspective of a licensed psychologist. Covers familiar material from a more clinical angle.

Fisher, Gary, and Cummings, Rhoda. *The Survival Guide for Teenagers with Learning Disabilities*. Minneapolis: Free Spirit Press, 1993.

Giannetti, Charlene, and Sagarese, Margaret. *The Roller-Coaster Years: Raising Your Child Through the Maddening Yet Magical Middle School Years*. New York: Broadway Books, 1997. This book covers all the emotional and mental aspects of the middle school years that I leave out in my book. Some included topics are: sibling rivalry, friendship and peer pressure, and sexual awakening. A classic and a highly recommended read for parents of middle-schoolers who want to focus in on the emotional development of their children. Extremely useful for teachers of middle-schoolers, as well, to keep them in touch.

Gross, David A. and Ira L. Extein. *A Parent's Guide to Common and Uncommon School Problems*. PIA Press, 1989.

Joslin, Karen. *Positive Parenting Your Teens: The A to Z Book of Sound Advice and Practical Solutions*. New York: Fawcett Books, 1997. A handbook that spells out how to deal with a multitude of teen problems by using dialogues and real-life examples.

Leana, Frank. *The Best Private High Schools and How to Get In: The A–Z Guide to the Private School Admission Process*. New Jersey: Princeton Review, 1998. A must for any student who is even thinking of applying to an elite private school. Mr. Leana covers over 140 private day and boarding schools and includes information on getting in as well as all the relevant information about each high school.

Levine, Mel, Dr. *Keeping a Head in School: A Student's Book about Learning Abilities and Learning Disorders*. Cambridge: EPS, 1990.

McCoy, Kathy. *Life Happens: A Teenager's Guide to Friends, Failure,*

Sexuality, Love, Rejection, Addiction, Peer Pressure, Families, Loss, Depression, Change, and Other Challenges. Perigee, 1996. Geared toward teenagers themselves and common crises they suffer.

Pipher, Mary Bray. *Reviving Ophelia: Saving the Selves of Adolescent Girls.* New York: Ballantine Books, 1995. Through case studies of teenage girls, Pipher highlights all the problems girls face during their adolescent years. A must-read for educators (and parents) who work with middle school-age girls. Chapters are arranged in a helpful checklist form.

Pope, Loren. *Colleges That Change Lives: 40 Schools You Should Know About Even If You're Not a Straight-A Student.* New York: Penguin, 1996. Loren Pope gears his book to students who don't fall into the overachieving, highly selective only crowd. I strongly recommend this book for parents of students who want an excellent college education and want to find out about non-Ivy alternatives that are first-rate.

——. *Looking Beyond the Ivy League: Finding the College That's Right for You.* New York: Penguin, 1996. Another well-written and easy-to-follow book by Loren Pope that is a must for parents of students who are aiming just below the top-tier colleges.

Quinn, Patricia, ed. *ADD and the College Student: A Guide for High School and College Students with Attention Deficit Disorder.* Washington D.C.: American Psychological Association, 1994. A reassuring guidebook for parents, students, and even college teachers who need to learn more about the problems that growing up with ADD presents. Lots of material relevant to succeeding in college is included as well.

Rice, Wayne. *Enjoy Your Middle Schooler: A Guide to Understanding the Physical, Social, Emotional, and Spiritual Changes of Your 11–14 Year Old.* Grand Rapids, MI: Zondervan Publishing House, 1994. A helpful book, but not as comprehensive as *The Roller-Coaster Years.* Geared toward parents.

Riera, Michael. *Surviving High School.* Celestial Arts, 1997. A book geared toward teenagers themselves rather than their parents. Mr. Riera covers a wide range of topics from "Being Gay" to "How to Get a Driver's License." He deals with difficult issues like drugs, alcohol, and sex. The author is a guidance counselor and gives lots of sound advice.

Stigler, James, and Stevenson, Harold. *The Learning Gap: Why Our Schools Are Failing and What We Can Learn from Japanese and Chinese Education.* New York: Touchstone Books, 1994. A fascinating read geared toward educators, parents, and administrators. The authors describe these Asian systems and how they compare to our own. We can lift many interesting ideas from these Asian systems.

Tracy, Louise Felton. *Grounded for Life: Stop Blowing Your Fuse and Start Communicating*. Seattle, WA: Parenting Press, 1994. An easy-to-read book geared toward parents who want to develop relationships with their teenage children.

Weiss, Lynn. *Give Your ADD Teen a Chance: A Guide for Parents of Teenagers with Attention Deficit Disorder*. Colorado Springs, CO: Piñon Press, 1996. A book geared toward parents that focuses on the academic difficulties ADD students face and ways to overcome those difficulties.

Yale Daily News. *The Insider's Guide to Colleges 1998 (24th edition)*. New York: St. Martin's Press, 1997. This is my favorite "insider" book of what it's like to be a student at the nation's top colleges. Since the descriptions are written by students, they tend to be quite on the mark.

About the Author

Michele A. Hernández graduated Phi Beta Kappa from Dartmouth College in 1989. After studying in Spain for a year at the Antonio de Nebrija Institute and learning four years of Latin in an intensive summer program at the Latin and Greek Institute of City University of New York, she earned a master's degree in English and comparative literature from Columbia University. At the Putney School in Vermont, she taught English and Spanish. For four years, she was an assistant director of admissions at Dartmouth College. Currently, she is the academic dean at a private school in south Florida. In her spare time, she can be found pursuing her scholarly interests, reading, listening to music, biking, rollerblading, international skeet shooting and playing with her three-year-old daughter Alexia.

Index